KING OF SPORT 4

by
Les King

ACKNOWLEDGEMENTS

*Les King would like to acknowledge
the help of the following:*

Olivia Wilkinson who did the type setting

Danny Nobbs who has kindly written the foreword

Lady Mayor Dianne Fernee

Wymondham Town FC

Dereham Town FC

Hardingham Cricket Club

My Wife Anita who unselfishly allows me to support sport and charity

Barkers Print & Design Ltd

Pictures and articles courtesy of Archant Newspapers

Kicking off for charity

Wymondham Regal first charity football team

Front Cover: Duncan Forbes and Jon Thaxton
               Les King and Violet May Royal lead the Wymondham Jubilee procession
               Mark Wilkinson, cricket match sponsor presents a cheque to Wendy Winterbottom
               Alan West, Sam Sexton, former Commonwealth Heavyweight Champion and Les King

Printed and published by Barkers Print & Design Ltd
Unit 7 Station Road Trading Estate, Attleborough, Norfolk

ISBN 978-0-9926670-1-6

CONTENTS

FOREWORD

"When asked by Les to write the foreword to this, his final book in the King of Sport series, I was honoured beyond words. Les King is known throughout Norfolk and beyond as one of the greatest supporters of sport in the county, in addition to being a larger than life character, as you will soon read. But it is his dedication and commitment to the charities which he supports that really does define the personality of this gentle giant.

I first met Les King when he was managing the Regal Cinema in Wymondham. Aged 12 (myself, not Les!), he towered over me as I queued up to watch 'Danny The Champion of the World' with my coins held tightly in my hand... only for Les to pat me on the head and usher me through free of charge. To say he was a flamboyant cinema manager is an understatement... who else other than Les could arrange for the Sally B bomber used in the film to fly over the town to celebrate the release of Memphis Belle, and get away with leading a white horse through the Regal to add another dimension to the Western that was playing!

17 years on, I was representing Great Britain at the 2008 Paralympic Games in Beijing in the F54 shot put event. I couldn't have achieved this without the amazing support of friends and family, including Les. Having had a motorbike accident at 17, I was left paralysed from the chest down and using a wheelchair, a big shock for someone whose life revolved around football and cricket but I approached my new situation with more determination than ever before. It is my ambition to once again represent my country, this time in the javelin, at the 2016 Paralympic Games in Rio De Janeiro, Brazil.

As you will soon read, Les King's charisma and love of sport has seen him alongside many of the sporting greats but without doubt, his driving force is his love of the charities he so actively supports. He introduced me to Star Throwers, and the tremendous work they carry out for those affected by cancer, several years ago, and this book, the proceeds of which will go directly into helping the charity, is a testament to his just name.

Danny Nobbs
Paralympic Athlete

INTRODUCTION

My first King of Sport book was foreworded by Norwich City legend Duncan Forbes. King of Sport 2 was foreworded by another Norwich City legend Bryan Gunn, and King of Sport 3 was foreworded by Norfolk boxing legend Jon Thaxton, this book is kindly foreworded by Danny Nobbs a Paralympic competitor. Danny has been a great help to me supporting my charity events.

This book is written in appreciation and thanks to all the good people who supported me at the Regal, also my charity football teams, cricket and boxing teams, also the support given to me at Chapel Road School, Attleborough for children with special needs, Ketts Lodge home for the elderly and now Star Throwers.

I became the first chairman of the Friends of Ketts Lodge home for the elderly. I had a good committee. We had fund raising events, which helped to get the resident's televisions.

I did my first charity event for Chapel Road school when I walked from London to Wymondham with my friends Alan Farrow, Bernard Daynes and Peter Steward. I became Chairman at the Friends of Chapel Road school about 28 years ago, I am still chairman and over the years we have had many hard working committee members giving their time to help the children there.

A year ago I became the first patron of local charity Star Throwers. Over the past two years I have arranged six events for them and they have all been well supported and have had good weather. The Lord above knows, that Star Throwers, in Wymondham, will be the best charity shop because so many good people support and care for people with cancer.

In my past three books, I wrote of local football, boxing, cricket and charity events. In the following chapters I will bring you up to date in sport, days out, holiday trips, wild life, the Queen's Jubilee and my charity events. Once again thank you to all the kind people who have given me support.

Les King

Les King

Where does one start when trying to talk about Les. I have known him since he took over the cinema. Les's untiring work with the young and sport has earned him immeasurable thanks and admiration. And that admiration was marked when at the Jubilee celebrations in 2012 Les was asked to be King of the celebrations. And now at nearly 80 Les has taken on yet another challenge and tirelessly raises funds for Star Throwers.

On a personal note I can never thank Les enough for taking my son on as a torch boy at the Cinema. It was something he really enjoyed and still talks of with fond memories.

Thanks Les.

Dianne

Dianne Fernee – *Mayor of Wymondham*

Lady Mayor Dianne Fernee with myself at a special lunch at Masterman Homes

Photograph by Jemma of JMA

CHAPTER 1

Park Farm Hotel
My second home

About 35 years ago when I ran the Regal cinema, the film reps would call and see me to book their films. They always asked if they could call on me last, they had a special reason as 5 or 6 wanted to stay at Park Farm Hotel. It suited me fine as after the film show myself and my wife would join them for a drink. Of course it had to be at the film company's expense, the drinks were about 3 shillings a pint, at that time the bar was downstairs so you could not have too much to drink as you had to climb the stairs to go home.

Mr Gowing seemed to be everywhere, driving the tractor on the farm, serving petrol at the fuel garage opposite the entrance to the hotel. Mrs Gowing made sure that the food and hospitality was first class. They were both hard working people and it was pleasing that their son, David had followed in his parents' footsteps. In those days, Mr Gowing let me take my lurcher dog in his harvest field. The corn was cut by tractor and binder. One evening while having a drink in the Feathers pub with Mr Gowing, he asked me if he treated me to half a lager would I take him to Barnham Broom as he wanted to see the sauna and the leisure set up. We met the manager, Alan Long, a lovely man and he gave Mr Gowing advice. Not long after our visit to Barnham Broom, Fitness Express were on their way to Park Farm. Over the next year or so there were a few transfers from Barnham Broom to Park Farm, the head chef who thinks he is the manager of Liverpool came, but the biggest transfer fee, not quite as much as Gareth Bale, was manager Richard Bond. Richard had a hard act to follow when he took over from Alan Long at Barnham Broom, he did well and now at Park Farm with his hard working staff and a lady called Sue who is always here there and everywhere, its down to her that the weddings and functions are first class. And then there's the 'Trolly Dolly' and 'Mrs Mop' all working hard. The hotel reception is very good and when guests leave they get mints to help them on their travels, I'm given a few mints as I do have to drive back to Wymondham...

I recently met Peter Gowing who now lives abroad, he always looks for me when he comes back to Park Farm. He cannot believe how the hotel and leisure centre have expanded to become Norfolk's best hotel and leisure centre, that's why I go there every day. I must write about the leisure centre staff at Park Farm, they are all good to me. There's Darren marathon runner, Joe footballer, Jack boxer, Tom rugby player, Kerrie lady footballer and Aaron personal trainer for the rich and famous (not me). It's good that the leisure team take part and support local sports. Thanks to my friend Gregg Baker of Fitness Express, Gregg helped out at the Olympics and was lucky to see Usain Bolt win both his races and get his gold medals. Gregg kindly gave me an Olympic badge which I dare not wear in case I lose it.

In 2010 I won the ten mile swimming race, and Gregg Baker kindly presented me with a small trophy, I won the same race the next year. This year 2013 there was a sponsored swim for Star Throwers with many members taking part including the leisure team. Over £2000 was raised and Park Farm had a new swimming champion as a special lady Marie England swam 21 miles and raised £550 for Star Throwers, I invited this lady to visit Star Throwers where she was presented with a special award from Doctor Henry Mannings.

The swimming champ with Kerrie, Gregg and Manager Darren Neale

I was honoured when I was to open the new steam room and sauna, later I cut the ribbon to open the new spa pool. Over the years there have been good staff at Park Farm, some have moved on to other fitness express centres. I shall remember my mate Richard, he is a big lad and always hungry, so most mornings on my way to Park Farm I would call in at Mervs to get a loaf of bread for Richard as he was fond of peanut butter and toast. There is a staff room and I also took coffee and became the canteen boy, that's why I get treated some days with a cup of coffee. There are many good and friendly members who like myself enjoy their visits there, even if it rains there's still plenty to do, to me it seems holidays are a thing of the past, you don't need to sit in traffic hold-ups or flight delays and queues at airports. I've been to Tenerife many times as you can read in the next chapter, Park Farm is now good enough for me.

Leanne   Nathan   Emily

Richard Bond, Steve Taylor, Les King, Aaron Johnson.
Les cuts the ribbon to open the New Spa Pool at Park Farm

Les King, Lady Mayor: Dianne Fernee,
Marie England receives her swimming medal from Dr Henry Manning

Les King and Rocky Watts shape up for the Heavy Weight title of Park Farm

Gregg Baker, Les King '10 Mile Swim Champion 2010', Steve Taylor

Scott Malcolmson, Les King cutting the ribbon on the
new sauna steam room and feature shower and Steve Taylor

Kerrie Smy presents a cheque for £2004.16 to Dr Henry Mannings of Star Throwers, which was raised by members and the Leisure Team by completing a sponsored swim.

Left - right: Tom West, Kerrie Smy, Les King, Daniel Lewin, Rob Lewin, Henry Mannings, Hazel Martin

Steve & Sue's wedding of the year at Park Farm

More than £120 was raised at a coffee morning at Park Farm

CHAPTER 2

Tenerife
And visits to The Pheasant Plucker

After I left my King of Sport shop it was agreed that as my wife liked the sun we should have some holidays. Many people recommended Tenerife as the sun shone all the year round and the drinks were cheap, also you could fly from Norwich Airport.

On a wet Tuesday morning we were on our way to the airport, and when we booked in I asked if I could have a window seat half way down on the left of the plane as you could get the best view. When the plane took off you could look down and see the city, and after a minute or so we were flying over Barnham Broom golf club where I am a life member. Not long after, the air hostess came round with breakfast. After four hours Mount Teide came into view there was snow at the top of the mountain which was higher than our plane was flying, and as the plane turned to land you could see the beaches and the hotels and a good view of the coastline. We flew low over the Golf Del Sur golf course and the sun was shining as we landed at Sur Reina Sofia airport, Tenerife.

A Dolphin Bus in Tenerife

After getting our luggage we went to the bus park where there were about 50 lovely buses to take people to their hotels. It was best to sit on the left side of the bus for the best view of the sea and hotels in Los Cristianos and Player De Las Americas before reaching our hotel Iberostar Bouganvilla Player. As we booked in I asked at reception if we could have a room with a sea view overlooking the pool about second or third floor. The hotel porter was Francisco who got to know well as I stayed at that same hotel about 20 times and I nearly always had the same room 243 or 245.

The next job was to find a bar that showed football and had a happy hour. We were lucky as about 50 yards across the road was The Pheasant Plucker (you have to be careful when you say that name). This bar had tables outside where you could sit and people

The Pheasant Plucker

watch, buses taking people to their hotels, airliners coming into land at the airport and cruise ships on the sea as they headed for Santa Cruz and happy hour was between 5 and 7pm when lager was 75p a pint, this suited me fine and Pheasant Plucker was to be my local when on holiday.

When it was known that Les King was in Tenerife, he would be at that bar and as it was happy hour he would buy you a drink. Many people came who I knew, Kenny and Connie Cooke, John Grady, and his daughter Caroline who was playing in the Tenerife golf open; Billy Farrow and Patsy, Bruce Cunningham and his wife Karen, Jon Thaxton and his mum and dad, John and Leigh Smith, Hop and his mates from Wymondham, friends who lived in Tenerife came to the bar also people who stayed in our hotel who we are still friends with, I did buy many drinks there but not after 7pm.

John Grady and daughter Caroline who was playing golf in The Tenerife Open

Pheasant Plucker Sandwiches

"Bad news - someones feelin' peckish"

Mr and Mrs David (Thatch) Ready came to Tenerife for their honeymoon. I think that Thatch had many honeymoons before that. They stayed in our hotel and I told the hotel reception Mr Ready was famous in Wymondham, well he played football. When they arrived Champagne was in their room, but they headed to the Pheasant Plucker soon after arriving and they spent more time there than they spent sunbathing.

When I am on holiday I do the same thing every day, get up at 6am, wash and shave, then take our towels to our sun beds, which

My friends the restaurant staff

are in the corner overlooking the sea. At 7am I go to the restaurant with my small tea pot and fill it with hot coffee to take to my wife who is still in bed. Then I go back to the restaurant and get a table so that I can see the sea and watch the sun rise. We have our breakfast at around 8am and around 9.30 I am ready to go to the pool taking with me my sun cream, a bottle of water, and a cheese roll which I had saved from breakfast. We would be by the pool all day then at 4pm I would go back to the room, have a shower and put on a clean shirt and trousers as you had to wear trousers in the restaurant in the evenings. At 5pm I made my way to the Pheasant Plucker, calling in to the shop next door where I would buy King Edward cigars which cost £2 for 5. I would get my table at the front and enjoy a few pints of lager, about 6pm my wife would join me for her drinks, and at 7pm we would go back to the hotel, to the restaurant, and on the way my mate on the hotel reception would get a cigar, and Domingos and Renaldo would also get a cigar as they kept us the same table overlooking the sea, and a bottle of wine would arrive at our table. To eat you could have prawns, fish steaks, ribs or a carvery; the food was very good.

Mr & Mrs at pool side

At about 9pm we would return to our room, sit on the balcony and have a few whisky and tonics, and watch the lights at down-town Player Las Americas as the night life began to take off. 10pm we would go to bed and watch the BBC news which you could get on our TV, then it was time to go to sleep.

Some days we did go out as Kenny and Connie Cooke who had a hire car picked us up and took us to a fish restaurant in Los Abrigos, where the planes flew very low as they came in to land. You could pick a fish to eat from a large tank as they swam, I did not like that, I just have fish and chips. Another day we had a trip out with John and Leigh Smith who also had a hire car, first we went to Los Gigantes where we walked round the harbour and watched the fish swimming, then we drove to the top of the mountain. I was scared as we climbed the narrow roads, it seemed miles below, I was glad when we reached Garachico it would be better coming back downhill.

I can remember one day before we were coming home I rang to book a taxi to pick us up from Norwich Airport. When I rang the taxi office a lad answered the phone and said "young Matt speaking is that you Les? Where are you? Las Americas, Tenerife, the Lad replied, don't worry Les, Cilla will pick you up in a half hour" this taxi was going to travel faster than Concord! We had many happy holidays in Tenerife, met many nice people who still keep in touch and send us Xmas cards. It seems that although I still keep busy, holidays are now a thing of the past.

My wife marked with an arrow at pool side. This photo was taken from our room
so you could see the view of Tenerife

The Lora Parque bus

CHAPTER 3

Las Vegas
The home of world boxing

Many years ago when I was a lad, I would get up and listen to the radio in the early hours of the morning broadcasting the big fights from America, the days of Joe Louis, Rocky Marciano and Sugar Ray Robinson, years later many friends of mine travelled to America to watch the big fight, somewhere I never thought I would go. Little did I know at the time that I would be going to the States to watch a world title fight.

During Xmas 1994 Herbie Hide, who I sponsored and helped during his boxing career, informed me that he was going to defend his world title against Riddich Bowe at the MGM Grand in Las Vegas and asked me if I was going to see the fight. Herbie said 'I bet you don't go'. Early in the New Year, my friend Steve Taylor said that if I decided to go to Las Vegas he would accompany me. A week before the fight, Steve Taylor picked me up in the early morning when it was still dark and we headed for Gatwick Airport. When we arrived, we parked the car about two miles past the airport and, with the car park at the end of the runway, I got a great view of the jets taking off. A bus then took us to our terminal and we made out way to the departure lounge. Our tickets and passports were checked and then we were allowed through; and from the departure lounge I was able to look over the airport. I had been on the outside watching the planes, and now I was on the inside.

We were to fly with Delta Airlines and I could see our jet, a TriStar, as the airport staff were getting it ready. Then we were told to proceed to the boarding gate and prepare to take our seats. My seat had been booked by a window, so that I could look out. The jet taxied to the runway and then made its take off. At last we were airborne and I looked down and saw a golf course. I could remember watching airliners when I had played golf there, but now I was taking off. On a screen at the front of the plane was a map of the route, which we were to fly, and a little arrow kept moving to show our position. The screen also showed the time of arrival at our destination. The hostess came round with the menu. We were now over the Atlantic and I looked out of the window for ships. Steve, who is not keen on flying, said that it would be better if we drank iced water. I looked at the screen, which indicated that there were 8 hours and 30 minutes to our arrival. There must have been twelve hostesses, who were working all the time, bringing food and drinks round and looking after us. A film came on the screen and I thought we would get nothing to eat while it was showing. When I woke up the film was over, and the flight map was back on the screen. The arrow had moved to just over halfway and it was then 4 hours and 55 minutes to our destination. We drank some more iced water, as I was keeping the miniature bottles of whisky, which I had been given on the plane, for my mum and dad. I thought that I would never get bored on an aeroplane but when you are in a confined space and there is not much leg room, the time seems to go by quite slowly. I did notice how the air hostesses all looked the same, with their hair and make-up just as immaculate as when they had started the journey. At last we were told to fasten our seatbelts as we were approaching Atlanta's Hartsfield International Airport, where we would have to change planes for our next destination, which was Fort Worth, near Dallas.

As we walked with our luggage from one terminal to another, I got an excellent view of the airport; and there seemed to be hundreds of jets. The plane, which we boarded to fly to Fort Worth, was a Boeing and once again I had a seat by a window, so I could look out across the wing and the engine. We were told to fasten our seatbelts and then the engines were started. I noticed smoke coming from an engine on my left and I told Steve, who looked worried. Then a woman in front of me noticed the smoke, and she shouted that the engine was on fire and that she wanted to get off the plane. The engines were stopped and the aircraft went silent. The captain told us that there was a problem and that there would be a delay. Passengers started to get off the plane and Steve said that we could catch a different flight.

We took our hand luggage and made for the front of the plane. We were told to go to a certain gate, so that we could take a different route to Las Vegas. We had around five minutes to get to the other side of the airport and I said to Steve "What about the luggage?" He replied, "Don't worry about that, we can buy some more when we get there!" We ran across the airport which was allright for Steve, who was fit, but I had a job to keep up with him. When we left England it had been cold, but now it was hot and I was sweating. We arrived just in time to board our next plane and we were told to change at Phoenix, Arizona, for Las Vegas. We were now in another Boeing, and I was glad to sit down as I was soaked in sweat. I asked a hostess about our luggage and was told "Take your seat, sir. We are about to take off." Once again I had a seat by a window, so at least I could see where we were going - if I only knew.

We were now heading for Phoenix, and looking out of the window, I said to Steve that the engines were all working. A hostess came round with drinks and again I enquired about our luggage. She just smiled at me and just asked me what I would like to drink. I could not make it out, that we were on a plane to Phoenix and our luggage was in a plane which should have been going to Fort Worth. There were only a few people on the plane to Phoenix, so our hostess sat down next to me and we had coffee together. Either she must have thought I was worried about my luggage, or she had never seen anybody like me before. She asked whether, in England I lived in the country and I replied, "Oh yes; I'm a country boy." She told me that she lived in Los Angeles and left home on a Monday morning to fly to and fro across America all week, returning home on a Friday. I had seen lots of air hostesses all day, and this one was the prettiest. I asked her if she was married and she replied that she was, and as she was away all week, her husband and her made up for it at the weekend. I replied "I can well understand that."

As we approached Las Vegas, the air hostess told us to look out of the window because it was such a fantastic sight. And how right she was! As the plane turned to land, all of the lights came into view and I had never seen anything like it before. The sky seemed full of lights of differing colours. We could see the M.G.M Grand, our hotel, and it seemed higher than the plane. Even Steve had found a window to admire the view. At last we had arrived and we did get our luggage, though I do not know how it got there before us. I looked at my watch, which said 7:15am but I had not changed it and in fact it was 11:15pm American time. From the moment Steve had picked me up, it had taken almost 28 hours to get to the McCarran International Airport in Las Vegas.

We took a cab from the airport to the M.G.M. Grand, which boasts over 5,000 bedrooms and is the biggest hotel in the world. There were over 15,000 seats in the M.G.M. Grand Garden, where Herbie's fight was to take place and the hotel also has a 33- acre theme park. We booked in and took the lift to our rooms. Later, we decided to look round the hotel and we discovered that in Las Vegas, you cannot tell if it is day or night. I had never seen so many fruit machines, and as we walked through the Hollywood and Monte Carlo casinos, I saw hundreds of people playing cards and roulette. On top of one fruit machine was a Harley Davidson motorcycle, and on top of another was a Porsche sports car, either of which you could win by just inserting a coin into the appropriate machine. I thought that this was no good to me, as if I had won either prize I would not have been able to get it home.

The next morning, I rose at 6:00am, while Steve was still asleep. I had a wash and a shave, and then made for the hotel entrance, which was already full of stretch limos. I went down to the bridge, which crossed the freeway, and watched the big trucks heading for Los Angeles. There were also plenty of jets coming in to land.

We visited the Oz Buffet for breakfast and found that it was about as big as a Marks and Spencer store. You pay about £3 and can help yourself to as much as you want, but there were so many different things to eat that I didn't know where to start. I had never seen so much food wasted as people were eating half what they had taken and were then going back to get something else. There must have been enough waste to feed hundreds of dogs. Herbie joined us for breakfast and was pleased to see me. He put his arm around me and remarked "I said you wouldn't come, but I always knew you would be here."

In the afternoon we decided to walk the famous Las Vegas Strip and it truly is a fantastic place. They advertised plenty of different dishes, but I did not get on too well with the food as it seemed to make me go to the toilet more than usual. We went past the Excalibur, where Wild Bill's sizzling steaks were being served. You could buy a steak and get a lobster free, have a steak and crab legs or a steak on a shrimp scampi. At the Golden Nugget, you could get a basket of fried shrimps and chicken with ribs of beef. At the Palomino, we could have called in and danced with the girl of our dreams or watched the biggest nude show in the states. But we kept on walking! We visited the Mirage, where we were met by white tigers at the entrance and saw five dolphins swimming in a pool. Next, we went to Caesar's Palace, where we sat down and had a coconut ice-cream. Opposite was Planet Hollywood, outside of which lots of people, who were shouting and screaming gathered. As I brought some more ice-cream, I asked the lady what was the attraction and she told me that Sylvester Stallone, who played the title role in the Rocky films, had just arrived. I said that we didn't need to see Stallone, as our mate was the real Heavyweight Champion.

We visited other places and looked in at the Luxor Hotel, before we went for tea. That evening, we had a drink with Richard Futter from Anglia T.V. and Kevin Lawrence from Radio Broadland.

On the Thursday, which was weigh-in day, Kenny Cooke, Maurice Graver and Mark, Maurice's son, who were all staying down the road, came to our hotel for breakfast with us. When we were all seated, Neville Downing arrived at our table and Maurice asked him, "How did you get here?" Neville replied, "I came on my bike. I have been here for six weeks and I've been sparring with Larry Holmes down at Ceasar's Palace." Kenny chipped in, "Neville, after all that you must be hungry, so you'd better sit down and have something to eat. There's plenty here for you." Mark Graver went round the food counter seven times! He started with cereals, fruit and pancakes with treacle, then went on to eggs, hash, sausages, and different fries, eventually finishing up with gateau and cream. Maurice said "My boy Mark can eat more than you Kingy." I replied, "So well he may, but when he's been at home you can't have given him enough grub".

We had invitations to the opening of the new Sugar Ray Leonard gymnasium, which is in downtown Las Vegas. Gary Delaney, Steve and myself boarded a bus which had been laid on from the hotel to the gym. Once again we passed the truck stop, where there were still plenty of big American lorries, and it took us about half an hour to get there. Sugar Ray Leonard gave a speech from the ring and Riddick Bowe was introduced, together with other personalities from the boxing world. Joe Frazier also climbed into the ring, and some youngsters put on exhibition bouts. I was lucky enough to be given a Sugar Ray T-Shirt and the former world champion signed it for me. I gave it to Steve for looking after me so well.

On fight night Barry Hearn came to the dressing room and remarked "It won't be long now ~" The message came through that Riddick Bowe was on his way to the ring and everybody stared to give Herbie encouragement. Herbie's entourage got ready to go, with Barry and Freddie at the front, Herbie in the middle and the rest of us behind so that nobody could touch Herbie. Barry said "Right we're on our way," and Herbie's song 'I am the one and only' blared out. When we entered the stadium it was packed and the ring was brightly lit. It seemed ages before Herbie reached the ring, but when he did, he received a great reception. Many famous people were introduced and then the announcements were made. The boxers were called to the centre of the ring by the referee Richard Steele and given final instructions about the rules. The bell sounded and it was round one.

Herbie got off to a great start, outscoring Bowe to win the opening round with ease. In round two, Herbie was still boxing well and Bowe was beaten to the punch. As Herbie came back to his corner, I really thought that if he kept to boxing he could win. In the third round, Bowe stared to come forward more and, near the end of the round, Herbie was hurt, but he was still ahead on points. However, the next three rounds were different and it seemed that Herbie had decided to slug it out with Bowe. In the fourth and fifth rounds, Herbie was knocked down five times, but on each occasion he got up and went after Bowe. Then in round six, after Herbie hit the canvas again, the referee stopped the fight. Riddick Rowe was the new Heavyweight Champion of the World.

In Herbie's dressing room after the fight, people were crying, Herbie's mum and brother Alan were very upset, then the defeated champion stood up and put his arms around me. He had tears in his eyes, but I told him that he had lost to the best heavyweight in the World and he had not let anyone down. Almost exactly a year earlier at Millwall, I had been in Herbie's dressing room for a champagne celebration where everyone was happy. Now it was disappointment, heartbreak and tears, but that is the difference between winning and losing in sport.

It was then 9:00pm in Las Vegas on a Saturday evening and then, after the fight, most people were making their way to the casinos. Steve and I were both disappointed and we decided to have an early night. As we were ging home the next day, we started to pack.

Early the next morning, I walked back to the MGM Grand Garden and the ring was still there. The cleaners were clearing up the rubbish and I went and sat at the back of the stadium. As I sat there, I wondered if I would ever return and whether Herbie would ever fight there again. I thought of the great champions who had fought there, like Julio Cesar Chavez, Larry Holmes, Mike Tyson and of course, Muhammed Ali. It can never be taken away from Herbie that he also topped the bill at the world,s most famous boxing arena.

Steve and I boarded flight number DL 644 and once again I had a seat by a window. I had a superb view of Las Vegas as the jet climbed up, and then we flew over the Nevada desert and the Grand Canyon. Later, we were told that we were flying over Louisville, the birth place of Cassius Marcellus Clay. By the time we reached Cincinnati, it was dark and, as we circled to land, I could see the famous lights. There seemed to be millions of them. We changed planes and from Cincinnati International Airport we were going to fly to Gatwick on a Tristar with Delta Airlines, and yes once again thanks to Steve's wife Kim I had a seat next to a window. On the flight, our menu for the main meal consisted of tossed spinach salad, a main course of fillet of salmon, or pasta and grilled chicken with apple flan for dessert. I slept most of the flight and as we approached Gatwick it was foggy so our landing was delayed. After touchdown and before we caught the bus to the car park I bought all the different newspapers to read the big fight reports. They all gave Herbie credit for his gallant effort.

A few years later I did travel back to Las Vegas and stayed at Circus Circus and went to the 50th anniversary of the American Air Force Air Show at Dallas Air base in the Nevada desert a few miles from Las Vegas, I also visited the Hoover Dam and the Grand Canyon on the famous fourmile strip there and nineteen hotels where you can spend a day in each so there is so much to see. You must also visit Freemont Street and for the best view of Las Vegas go to the top of the Stratosphere. I think that everybody would enjoy a once in a lifetime trip to Las Vegas.

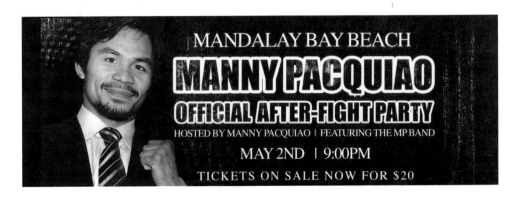

FOR THE LAST THREE DECADES, LAS VEGAS HAS DOMINATED THE FIGHT GAME

Myself and former World Champion
Evander Holyfield

Myself, Kenny Cooke, Neville Downing, Maurice Graver, Mark Graver and Steve Taylor
at Breakfast in Las Vegas

CHAPTER 4

Hardingham
Where I have spent many happy days

When my mum was a young girl she lived at Low Street, Hardingham. She would walk in all weathers to the school there over a mile away. After leaving school she worked at Hardingham Hall for Sir Bartle and Lady Edwards where she was well treated.

When my mum and dad were married and I grew up we lived at Lincoln Avenue, Hingham, just off the Hardingham Road, ten minutes bike ride to Hardingham. When I was about 12 years old and after school I would get on my bike and head for Hardingham passing Vincent's Farm on my left, Cut Bush Farm on my right. Then I would get to the George family at Nordelph Corner where there was a big family of all boys, Dick, Wally, Wriggy, Siddey, Joe, Roger and Bob. We would play football there, go in the harvest field and Mrs George was always cooking so there was always something to eat.

I had a lurcher dog and when we went in the harvest field, Dick Benton drove the tractor and Frank Adcock would ride on the binder. Sir Bartle made sure that all the rabbits and hares, when caught would have to be put on the binder to be shared with all the workers on the estate, but I always had a rabbit or hare to take home. On Saturday mornings I would help Bertie George at Vincent's Farm. We spread the manure on the fields with a garden fork, I would get a dozen eggs for my work. My dad had the best garden in Hingham and we had plenty of vegetables. He would catch fish from Scoulton Mere. I do have mates who go sea fishing but they don't catch anything.

We swam in the moat pit, but the best place to swim was in the river near the railway station. If you could not swim you got thrown in the river, that way you soon learnt to swim. As we swam in the river we could watch the steam trains puffing past. At that time, I did not think that in years to come I would be a train driver, stopping at Hardingham station.

After leaving school, I would go brushing at the hare coursing meetings at Kimberley and the shoots at Hardingham.

We had a lads football team at Hardingham ran by postman Horrie Elvin. I was in the team and when we played away in the Dereham area we would bike to the station, put our bikes in the guard's van, and travel by steam train to our away games.

I used to bike to Hardingham village hall to the youth club. I had a girlfriend named Sylvia, we had a cuddle under the big oak tree on the cricket pitch out field, this girl wore big glasses and each time I kissed her they scratched my nose. When I told her about this she said "I will take my glasses off but I'm not taking anything else off." The big oak tree is still there today, and when playing cricket if the ball hits the tree the batsman gets a four but there was no score for me when courting under the big tree.

My nanny and grandad Barker moved from Low Street to Beeches Lane just behind the cricket pitch. The Websdales, Elvins, Georges and Hubbards were big families living at Hardingham and taking part in the village sports teams.

After brushing at Kimberley coursing I had my own greyhound and became a member of the coursing club and my dog did well. At that time I lived at Kimberley and after roadman Horry Jones made me a dog cart which went behind my bike, I biked miles so my dog could compete at coursing meetings. I also had a good lurcher dog and friends of mine who also had good lurchers were Michael Long with his Pinkie, Norman Durrant with Rider, Eddie Manning, Moppy Smith, Duggie Nunn, Ali Bayles, David Filby and Mick Ramanous. I can remember when Ali Bayle's lurcher was chasing a hare, the hare ran down the road as a bus came heading for Hingham, the hare went under the bus, the dog hit the front of the bus and the radiator burst. The hare and dog ran on but the bus had to be replaced. Who would have thought a dog could put a bus out of action.

I told my lurcher friends to stay clear of the Kimberley and the Hardingham Estates. Sid Carter was the gamekeeper at Kimberley and Frank Havis at Hardingham, two of Norfolk's most respected gamekeepers. When the fete was held at Hardingham Hall I would go there and gamekeeper Frank Havis would be there and would buy me a cup of tea and a cake and would say sit there so I know where you are. Frank was a lovely man I liked him very much. Frank need not have worried as my dad told me as Henry Edwards was good to him giving him firewood for his Steam Engine, don't shoot pheasants on the Hardingham estate, and I never did.

I did watch the burning down of Hardingham Mill not far from where I learnt to swim. This was done for the film 'The Shuttered Room' which was shown many times at my Regal Cinema.

A few years later Henry Edwards asked if I would open the Hardingham Fete, which was now held on the cricket field. I was pleased to do this and when Henry introduced me he said some kind words about me, I thought I am getting back in the good books. Over the years the Fete at Hardingham has become the best village Fete in Norfolk. There is even a special train running from Dereham Station to Hardingham to bring people to the Fete. More recently my friend Lizzie Dann who now lives in Hardingham has helped Henry at the Fete. I did teach Lizzie how to play golf, we both went to Newmarket Races as guests of Bedford Lodge Hotel where we mixed with all of the posh guests but between us we never backed a winner. On the way home, near Thetford, I asked if we could stop in the lay-by. Lizzie agreed to stop as she was driving, but she said "You are not doing nothing." Once again like under the big tree at Hardingham cricket pitch I had failed to score.

I would take my dad and my friend Billy Mann the mushroom farmer from Wicklewood and we would go in my jeep to the harvest fields at Hardingham. We would sit there and watch the big combine cut the corn and we would see hares, rabbits, foxes and even deer. When hares and rabbits come out of the corn they are lost as if they had lived in the cornfield and they were now in new surroundings. Now with the dust from the combines, taking your dog to the harvest field is a thing of the past. In the winter we go to the shoots, I can sit in my jeep and as the beaters move through the woods the wild life comes out the other end; hares, rabbits, foxes and even deer and nothing can be shot on the ground which is good, the pheasants fly high and I can tell you more get away than get shot.

As Life President of the cricket club I go there most matches and as we sit watching the cricket I listen to people talking. A.A tells me that he built three houses in a week, Vernon talks of his trips in the camper van and my mate Sam Harris, now 93, tells of how he painted Norwich Union, painted City Hall, was captain of a ship that sailed to Japan, then he will show you photographs of the girls in Japan which we have seen many times, but Sam sets a fine example of how when you grow old, you can still enjoy watching local sport. Sam will always be made welcome at Hardingham.

I then listen to my mate Terry Elvin who I have known for over 60 years. He tells me the best place to buy sea food, how to cook a ham hock, when he goes to the fish stall at Hingham and tells you what to buy, shoots and eats three rabbits a week, if you listened to Terry, you would think that he feeds half of Hardingham. He makes me angry when he keeps telling me you cannot keep looking back, I disagree with him as I think of my friends Duncan Forbes, Dave Stringer and Kevin Keelan at Norwich City, Joe Louis, Rocky Marciano, Muhammad Ali all great boxers, our teams playing football at Hardingham, the good teams at Hingham playing at the Ladies Meadow, and the years when Hardingham's cricket team were league champions for several seasons.

Those days of sport should never be forgotten.

I must say that the cricket pitch now looks the best I have seen for many years thanks to Dale Watson and his lad Dylan.

Perhaps after reading this chapter you can see why I have spent many happy days at Hardingham.

Two good friends of mine Michael Long and Arthur Nudds enjoyed their visits to Hardingham

OFFICIAL CARD

Admission By Card £5   Including Owners And Trainers

KIMBERLEY & WYMONDHAM COURSING CLUB

(Under N.C.C. Rules)

President: Mrs D.M. Hambro

First in Slips 9.00 a.m. Sharp.

Coursing at

Hardingham

by kind permission of Messrs Edwards, Hardingham Farms Ltd.

Thursday 17th February 2005

Judge: Miss A. Filkins   Slipper: Mr W. Drew

The cover of the programme of the last hare coursing meeting in the area.
It seems hare coursing is now a sport of the past.

David Pike, combine driver and Hardingham Estate's gamekeeper, David Johnson with a dead fox which was shot in the harvest field. Foxes must be shot because they destroy so much young wildlife

Gamekeeper David Johnson, My Dad George, and my mate Billy Mann

Hares in the harvest field

CHAPTER 5

BOXING
Norwich Lads Club
and Norwich and District Ex-Boxers Association

The Lads Club now have a first class gym at the Hewett School and is still the best club in Norwich. Over the years many have worked hard to keep the club going. I have wrote of those people in my past books, Alan Weston, Paul Ferguson, Alan Nicolls have now taken a back seat. I am life patron and still give the club my support.

The club made history when Michael Walsh became Norfolk's first A.B.A. Champion. Sam Sexton, Nathan Dale, Danny McIntosh, the three Walsh brothers all past members of our club are now doing well in professional boxing. In the past Jon Thaxton and Herbie Hide became champions which is a credit to all the good coaching at Norwich Lads Club.

I can go back to the days of Ginger Sadd when he topped the bill at the Corn Hall in Exchange Street. I boxed for the Attleborough boxing club over 60 years ago when Joe Bennett ran the club. Now the club is one of the best in the country with a hard working committee and a first class gym. In 1957 I boxed Ginger Sadd over four rounds at the Woman's Institute Hall in Wymondham, a few months later I beat Ray Bracey there, this was the last boxing show ever in Wymondham. My friend John Culyer who did so much for local sport helped me when I started the boxing club at Dereham and I became a sponsor at Norwich Lads Club. Dick Sadd and Chris Scott brought a young lad to the club, a friend of my son Sean, he was Herbie Hide. They both started boxing for the club. Sean won his first seven fights then retired. Herbie, who I sponsored went on to be British and World Heavy Weight Champion. I sponsored many boxers at the Lads Club, I am glad I did, as most did become boxing champions.

In October 2009 Jon Thaxton retired from boxing, he was a professional for 17 years, I spoke with Jon that evening and we both agreed he had made the right decision. I can remember when he first came to Norwich Lads Club, he was about 13, a friendly and ambitious lad, he met Dick Sadd the head coach and his boxing career was underway. Like so many before him I could fill this chapter with names of so many boxers who started there and became champions, that's why Norwich Lads Club is the most famous club in East Anglia. On December 9th 1992 Jon had his first professional fight. In boxing there are always heart-breaking days and unfair decisions, Jon had his fair share of these set-backs, but he overcame them and went on to become World Champion, European Champion and British Champion. No one in sport deserved to be a champion more so than Jon. He fought the best in the world, what a close fight he gave Ricky Hatton at Wembley. You will have read in the press of his great fights. I am proud of him as I know all the charity work he had done and he has helped me in many charity events, and his family have worked so hard to support him. As I have said many times, my friend Duncan Forbes is a Norwich City football legend, now Jon Thaxton has become Norwich's boxing legend.

Over the years many people have kindly sponsored the Lads Club, but for the past several years the Evening News thanks to my friend Matthew Chambers, have sponsored our club, and now our Ex Boxers Association have our monthly meetings at Sam Sextons K. O. Sports Diner. I was honoured to be invited to heavyweight boxing champion Sam Sexton's opening of his new K.O. Sports Diner, the former Pat's Café on Hall Road. Jon Thaxton, the three Walsh brothers, Jackson Williams, Chris Lakey, Steve Adams and Derek James from the local press all came and gave Sam their support. It's a place all boxing fans must visit as the boxing photos and memorabilia were the best that I have ever seen and the food was so good I became the first in the new diner to go round twice. I am pleased and so are so many others that Sam's new diner is making my charity, Star Throwers their charity fundraiser.

With my mate Chris Lakey keeping you up to date with his reports of boxing in the local press and Derek James with the past of local boxing history also in the local press, that's why I have less to write and can use more photos in this chapter, thanks to them and I still have to treat them to breakfast at Sam's Diner.

A group of lads and club officials with a club sponsor Shaun O'Brian at the club gym

Award winning boxers show off their trophies at Norwich Lads Club's presentation evening. *Front row from left:* Robert Ferguson, Ryan Winson, Craig Weston, Paul Ferguson, Melly Dunthorne and Tom Baugh. *Back row from left: treasurer* Alan Weston, *secretary* Ian Munday, *chairman* Les King, Francis Ampofo, Jon Thaxton, and *vice-chairman* Sean King

A happy group of Norwich Lads Club officials and president Kenny as he receives a cheque from a kind lady sponso

Who is the Teddy Boy minder in the background when Muhammad Ali came to Norwich?

Norwich Mayor Roy Blower (right) with Lads Club patron Les King

Bruce Cunningham, ABA Boxing Champion Michael Walsh & Kenny Cooke

Myself with Jon Thaxton & Trainer Graham Everitt

My son Sean with Anthony Ogogo

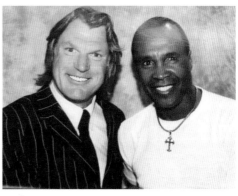

Sean with Sugar Ray Leonard

The opening of the Lads ABC
at the Hewett School

Les King Club Patron & Hon Life member being
presented a cheque of sponsorship from Matthew
Chambers, Assistant Head of Sport at the Evening
New & EDP. The Club is very appreciative of the
Evening News continual support.

Les King with long time mate George Blazeby

Mrs Jean Culyer, Myself and Andy Culyer with the
John Culyer Club Man of the Year Award

This photo was taken at the Dick Futter Memorial Show.
These lads have supported local boxing for many years.
Left - right: Charley Betts, Billy Royal, Bev Chapman, Michael Long, Jumma Hunt, Les King,
David Ridgeway, Sean King, David Wilson & Kenny Buckenham

Left - right: Ken Brown, Harry Surruys, Francis Ampofo, Myself, & Dave Boy Green
at a boxing event at Lakenham Leisure

PRIDE OF NORWICH: From left, Ampofo, Cassie Jackman (world No. 1 ladies squash player), King, Green, and former Norwich City football captain Duncan Forbes

NORWICH Lads ABC staged a presentation night recently which also served as an opening ceremony of the Les King Gym.

Club headquarters at Lakenham Sports & Leisure Centre have been renamed in honour of long-serving chairman King as a "thank you" for all his hard work over the years.

Club coach Alan Weston told local paper, the *Evening News*, "Les has been a key figure in the success of this club and helped lift it off its knees since the move from King Street. He's a real character around the gym and everyone respects what

Les is king for a night

he has done." Making it a great night for Les was that he was also celebrating his 70th birthday.

Eastern Counties hero Dave "Boy" Green of Chatteris was on hand to present Les with a copy of his recently-published biography *Fen Tiger* (written with Bob Lonkhurst).

Former pro champion Francis Ampofo, who now lives in Norfolk, joined Green in giving medals to Norwich Lads' carded boxers and certificates to the junior section.

Awards went as follows: Best Senior – ABA semi-finalist and England rep *Sam Sexton* (presented by Paul Ferguson); Best Junior – *Robert Ferguson* (presented by Clive Campling); Dick Sadd Memorial Award – *Caine Brunning* (presented by Steve Sadd); Culyer Clubman of the Year – *Alan Weston* (presented by Jean Culyer); Chairman's Award – *Jamie Lewis* (presented by Dave Boy Green); Jack Royale Memorial Award – *Frank Sictorness* (presented by Billy Royal); Most Improved Boxer – *Rolly Gatward*.

Enjoying themselves at our Club Awards Night: 3
Ex-Lads' Boxers who as professionals topped
the bill throughout the country. *Left - right:*
Len Jarvis, Tony Webster and Clive Campling

Jon Thaxton, Jon Brazil *best boxer of the night award* and
Phil Ward *Auto Aid* Trophy kindly given by Phil Ward

Left - right: Andy Berwick *Norwich Lads',* Les King *Chairman,* Debbie Cooke *Dolphin Travel,*
Chris Arabje *Marvels Lane winner* & Gordon Mallett

Craig Weston was voted Norwich Lads' ABC's boxer of the year by the
Norwich & District Ex-Boxers Association. He is pictured receiving his trophy
from Ex-Boxers President Les King also in picture are Norwich Lads' ABC Officials

Herbie on top of the world

Herbie Hide with long-time friend Les King

Andy Roydon was voted Norwich Lads' boxer of the year by Norwich and District Ex-Boxers' Association. He is pictured receiving his trophy from Ex-Boxers' president Les King, who is also Lads' Chairman. Also pictured *left - right:* Johnny Pipe, Bev Chapman, Dick Sadd, Les King, Jimmy Carter and Tony Webster

Standing left - right: Jack Wakefield, Paul Gamble, Tony Webster, Gordon Ferguson, Billy Baines, Shaun Jones, Jimmy Carter, George Blazeby, Harold Loveday & Les Bultitude. *Seated:* Albert Brighton, Johnny Pipe, Les King & Dick Sadd.

Andy Smith, Don Cockell, John Culyer, Boy Green, Duncan Forbes at Culyer Sports

President Kenny Cooke, *Hon. Vice-President* Jon Thaxton, *Vice-President* Bryan Gunn & *Chairman* Les King

Left - right: Danny Shutts, Tristian Lemay & Damien Lemay

Kenny Cooke *President* and Les King *Chairman*

At the Clarence Harbour, Chucky Robinson, Kenny Taylor, Johnny Pipe, Clive Campling, Len Jarvis, Dick Futter, Dick Sadd

Tudor Hall Night Club stages a Charity Cabaret in aid of Norwich Lads Club

Mr John Donnelly co-director of Tudor Hall *left.* Chucky Robinson with boxing gloves draped around him that were bought in auction by Mr Eddie Harvey *right,* proprietor of Marlborough Hotel Stacy Road, jointly with Mr John Grady, Norwich builder, Bev Chapman *centre rear.*

October 1971, the great Muhammad Ali visited Norwich.

New diner really packs a punch

By DEREK JAMES

Picture:
STEVE ADAMS

It's a new home for men who have packed a hefty Norfolk punch over the years – our boxers.

This proud city and county has produced some highly talented members of the noble art over the decades – from Jem Mace and Ginger Sadd to Jon Thaxton and Sam Sexton.

Times have changed but the bond of friendship between these men, and they come in all shapes and sizes, remains as strong as ever.

Only those who have ever stepped into the ring, in front of thousands of fans or in an empty hall, will know how that feels. The enormous respect you have for your opponent.

Because once the command "seconds out" is heard and the bell rings, you know you are on your own. It is time to stand up and be counted.

The Eastern Area Ex-Boxers, Norwich and District, Association, has done much good work over the years – keeping an eye out for former boxers – but in recent times many of their members have died.

Late last year they lost John Pipe, Pat Howard and Kenny Cooke, leaving just three originals left – Les King, Len Jarvis and Reg Harris.

"We had to decide whether or not to keep going," explained Les, the former boxer, railwayman and cinema boss.

The opening of a new café by Norwich boxer Sam Sexton – the KO Sports Diner on Hall Road, Norwich – helped them to make the decision to carry on and reach out to the boxing world.

"We had a meeting earlier this month and decided that we must keep going," said Les.

The new team comprises of president Sam Sexton, chairman Les King, treasurer Len Jarvis and secretary Reg Harris.

The new committee members are: Jon Thaxton, Graham Everitt, George Blazeby, Tommy Webster, Sean King, Mark Atkins and Mark Whitworth.

"We want to see as many boxers, all those from the Lads Club over the years, as possible to come and join us and the café is the perfect place to meet," said Les.

"All former boxers will be very welcome."

■ The club will meet on the first Sunday of the month, and the next time will be on Sunday, April 7.
■ derek.james@archant.co.uk

MEETING PLACE: Sam Sexton outside KO's Sports Diner on Hall Road, Norwich, with fellow boxers, past and present. The café will be a meeting place for them to get together.

BACK IN THE DAY: Ginger Sadd and Les King in the ring for a exhibition bout in 1957.

CLUB THAT TURNED LADS INTO MEN

From no-holds barred brutal and bloody prize-fights on Mousehold featuring the likes of Jem Mace and Licker Pratt to three-minute rounds under strict rules and regulations – boxing has changed beyond all recognition over the years.

The home of Norwich boxing became the Norwich Lads Club and it was in 1918 when a young boy stepped forward and took a swipe at a punchball.

He had come in off the city streets to see what was on offer at the Lads Club, the first club of its kind anywhere in the world.

He and his mates gathered round the punchball and watching them was a big man with a vision – his name was John Henry Dain and he was the Chief Constable of Norwich.

These were the days of birching and Borstal when community relations could be summed up by a "clip round the lug."

Dain was a man with pioneering and

revolutionary views. He reached out to the boys of Norwich, setting up the first youth club to be run by the police. It worked a treat.

Although there were a host of activities at the club which moved to

King Street, it was boxing that it was most famous for. The lads were turning into men – boxing taught them how to keep their temper, respect others and it gave them a purpose in life.

In the 1930s home secretary J R Clynes visited Norwich to see the club where more than 8,000 boys has been members.

"It costs £60 a year to put a boy in Borstal and keep him there. Far better and cheaper to keep him out," he said.

Norwich Lads Club gained a reputation for being very handy boxers and one boy came out of the backstreets of Norwich to become a hero – Arthur "Ginger" Sadd.

He went on to become a boxing legend and his brother Dick later set up the Ex-Boxers Association. They inspired a generation of boxers and devoted so much of their time to helping other lads become the boxers of the future.

Local boxing fraternity prepare for a double celebration

There is a double anniversary for local boxing this weekend as two of the sport's established organisations celebrate their history.

The Norwich & District Ex-Boxers Association is 40 years old, while the Norwich Lads Club is still going strong at 95 years of age. Tomorrow, the great and the good of the sport will be meeting at the KO Sports Diner in Norwich – with owner, heavyweight

fighter and Ex-Boxers Association president Sam Sexton in charge of catering.

"Our Ex-Boxers Association was started by Dick Sadd and the first meeting was held at the West End pub, where Ginger Sadd's daughter was the landlady," explained Les King, the honorary life president.

Les can reel of a who's who of local boxers, many of whom began

life at the Lads Club.

"It is where all our champions, both amateur and professional, started their boxing careers, from Ginger Sadd, Jon Thaxton, Herbie Hide, Jackson Williams, Danny McIntosh, Sam Sexton, the three Walsh brothers, Scott Moises and Nathan Dale – and of course Graham Everett," he said.

"The Lads Club opened in 1918 and the founder was John Henry Dain, the chief constable of Norwich. For many years the police helped run the club to

keep the youngsters from roaming the streets of Norwich, which is still our aim.

"For the past 95 years the Lads Club has been a credit to Norwich and for the past 40 years our Ex-Boxers Association have kept together to remember and never forget all the boxers who did Norwich proud."

It always seem to me that the boxing fraternity treats its ex-members better than most. I may be wrong, but they do seem to be a very close bunch.

CHAPTER 6

Football

In my past King of Sports books I wrote of many local Players and Clubs, from me playing and being Captain of Hingham just after leaving school, then playing for Wymondham Town before joining the Army where I played for the Royal Norfolks then the Essex Regiment in Korea. I did serve in Korea when I was 18 and as I write this people are having reunions as it's the 60th anniversary of the Korean War. When I came home I gave my mum my two active service medals. I played football again for Wymondham then Dereham, I then had many happy years at Dereham Wanderers. On Thursdays I played in the Norwich Railway team where I worked at Thorpe Station. Sunday I would play for Hingham, I then played at Deopham playing my last game when I was 60 years old.

By that time I had been supporting local clubs as either Chairman or President or Sponsor. Many years ago when I was Chairman of the Ex Service Men's Club, where I was Chairman for many years, (the club's longest Chairman ever), a lady press reporter Christine Cunningham called to see me, she was a good looking lady we became friends. She said that many people and Wymondham Town FC Committee would like me to become Chairman of the club in their Centenary year. I did become Chairman and am now Life President of the club. I was also Life President and Sponsor of Wymondham Sunday. I am Life President of Wroxham FC also Morley Village FC. I became President of all the youth teams in Wymondham where young lads are encouraged to play football. I am Vice President of other local clubs also Dereham Town FC. Since I met that lady press reporter it seems she set me on my way in local football. I often see Christine when watching cricket at Swardeston, I have invited her to come to my club at Hardingham, we could have tea under the big oak tree which is still there.

I was Chairman here at Wymondham in our Centenary year, we won the league that year. Then I went to Wroxham for a small fee. I became Life President and spent 25 happy years there. I did the raffle for over 20 years, received clubman of the year award, and the stand is named The Les King Stand in recognition of my support to the club. The club won many awards, league and cups and to think Bruce Cunningham had a team which won the Jewson Premier League 6 times in 8 years was the best. No one will ever better Bruce's record in local football.

The league was much stronger then, as ten teams have now moved on to a higher grade of football. But in May 2009 Wroxham did well to reach the F.A. Vase final at Wembley. No one will ever work harder in football as Kenny Cooke for Wroxham; Kenny arranged all of the buses and tickets for supporters with the help of Colin Hazel. We had our lunch at Wembley where Royalty sit, we watched the game from the Royal box, this was something that Kenny thoroughly deserved to see his team play at Wembley. Wroxham lost but they did well to get there, it was pleasing to see that many local people had a good day out. I sold over 100 tickets in Wymondham and when you look from the Royal Box and see these people it's special. A week after Wembley Kenny Cooke resigned as treasurer and other officials and sponsors left the club. To me Wroxham F.C. will never be the same without Kenny Cooke at the helm. It's a long way from Wembley football stadium back to football here at Wymondham. There's some good lads at Wroxham who are still my friends, but I think more people are now watching local football where players pay to play. That's why we get good support here at Wymondham.

People ask me about Wymondham teams over the years, and I can remember many good teams here starting with Fred Hall's 1954 team from the old Norfolk and Suffolk League, there was George Barker, Neville Royal, John Barham, David Hagan, Vic Barrett, Ken Percival, Percy Bunn, Eric Darkins and Kenny Ready. Fred Hall was a lovely man and when I worked at Wymondham Station on the Shunter Steam Engine, yes there was a steam engine, at the station in those days, Fred came on his bike and signed me from Hingham, no seven days notice and no transfer fees in those days. That was over 50 years ago now you see why I would like to see football at the Kings Head Meadow for many years to come.

In 1971 Derek Turner's team were League Champions, Derek was the playboy type always smart, he was a good footballer and his team was possibly the best ever, the lads in that team were Neil Tranter, Vernon George, John Eaglen, Barney Howes, Mel Gladwell, Bernie Sayer, Richard Carter, Evan Hall, Dave Reeves, Dick Bulcock and Dave Preston.

Writing of our best teams of the past, our team in the centenary year was the best ever. The president was William Armstrong, chairman was Les King, secretary Mick Utting, press man Peter Steward and manager and goalkeeper Dave Bedson. The team was Richard Gostling, Maurice Stafford, Leo Parke, Adie Lee, Paul Brown, Steve Matthews, Colin Glover, Peter Cunningham, Kevin Bugg, Ian Quirk, Paul Winter, Kevin Ready joined later and this team became League Champions, over 200 came and watched our home games and we even beat Wroxham in the Senior Cup. Saturday evenings we would all visit the Chinese restaurant in Damgate Street, Mr Lamb or Mr One Hung Low as some players called him, would charge us £5 for wine and all you can eat if we won, that's why we were in there almost every Saturday. Some players tell me that was the best season they enjoyed in football, we had over 15 on the committee and it seemed all of the town supported the club. It would be good to get back to those days.

More good teams of the past, Steve Foyster's Wymondham Sunday 1984 League Champions had to be the best Sunday side ever. They remained unbeaten in the League all season, and only twelve players were used. As we had large crowds, it was my job to go round with the collection box, Chairman Derek Minns made sure all of the players had half time oranges. Robert Thorpe was our secretary, the best clubman ever and Muskie our linesman was the best in Sunday football. The Players in that great team were Mike Phoenix, Steve Phoenix, Steve Cracknell, Paul Brown, Andy Johnson, Nigel Lee, Rick Henwood, Barry Miller, Steve Brown, Leo Parke, Tim Saunders, Kevin Piper and Nick Foyster. After the games at the Rec we would all go to the Feathers where landlord Eddie Aldous made us welcome with chips, biscuits, onions and cheese (there were big mice). In those days, Eddie was very good to us as he was to many people and later became the club chairman. As I drive past the Rec, I feel sad there is no football there now, so that's why I hope football can be kept at the Kings Head Meadow for years to come.

When my friend Bryan Gunn was Manager at Norwich City I asked him if he would bring his team to play Wroxham in a friendly game. Bryan smiled and replied "you don't want much do you? I will have to think about it". A few days later Bryan rang me and said Wroxham could come and play a City side at Colney training ground one afternoon in the week. After speaking to the then Wroxham Manager David Batch, he stated this could not take place as most of our players have to work. I told Bryan Gunn we could not play at Colney, but we would like to play at Carrow Road, we would not want expenses just something to eat and drink after the game. Bryan smiled and said "just for you Les you can bring Wroxham to play at Carrow Road with an evening kick off. I was proud that evening as with other Wroxham officials we sat in the Directors box, a strong City side beat Wroxham 4-0. Thanks to Bryan Gunn we all had an enjoyable evening.

In the early days of Bryan and Sue Gunn's Leukaemia charity I did help and still have the shirt I was presented with. Bryan has helped me many times in my charity events. When John Bond was Manager at Norwich City he would bring his players on Friday evenings to the Regal Bingo. I went to Carrow Road to see Ken Brown and Mel Machin who agreed to bring a Norwich City team to the King's Head Meadow to play the Town in our Centenary year, about 1250 people watched this game, City who brought a strong side won 3-1. Even Chairman Robert Chase came, and my friend Duncan Forbes bought a round of drinks, a very rare treat as Duncan would say you had to have short arms and deep pockets. How football has changed it seems its more about money than football. The millions Real Madrid paid for Gareth Bale and all the thousands players are paid.

When I had my Olympic transport company, in the summer close season City players Duncan Forbes, Roger Hansbury, Billy Steele and Welsh international David Jones came and helped me and of course Duncan had to be foreman. I knew of other City players getting part time jobs. When I lived at Kimberley I did get the blame from gamekeeper Sid Carter of shooting his pheasants on the estate. Recently I met ex city players Kevin Keelan and Bill Punton, Kevin now lives in Tampa Bay, Florida and when he was here on holiday I met him and Bill Punton and they admitted as being the Kimberley poachers, which I was blamed for, and they never got caught as being footballers they could run fast.

I was sorry to hear John Bond had died, John was a good friend of mine and he helped me as he did many others, when I had my removal firm Olympic Removals, John gave me the job of removal for many famous players coming or leaving Norwich City. His coach John Sainty played for my Wymondham Sunday team and after games John Bond, his wife and several other players, I and my wife Anita would have Sunday lunch at the Doric in Attleborough, but before lunch we would meet at the Windmill for a few drinks. George Gill, who kept the pub at the time, would try and pick the team for the next game and I would always say don't forget my friends Duncan Forbes and Roger Hansbury. In fact, John thought the world of Duncan and Roger and they never let him down. I went with John on the team bus for some away games and flew with the team to Liverpool sitting next to Sir Arthur South and Norwich won. When John left for Manchester City, I moved him there and he even sent me tickets for games there and we would go in the player's lounge. I first saw John play at West Ham, not only was he a first class player he became a great footballer manager.

I have wrote of the death of my friend John Bond, now I write of the passing of another gentleman and a fine ambassador of sport, Alfie Fincham who everybody respected in Attleborough. When I met Alfie he was always happy with a smile on his face and made you welcome. Credit and thanks to Andy Gardiner for his fine tribute to Alfie in the local press and to Mick Money for his kind words and his admiration of Alfie. Both Andy and Mick were among the hundreds of youngsters who Alfie encouraged to take part in local sport. In his younger days, Alfie would mark out the pitch and wash the football kits for many teams. In later years he would help with the fund raising and work hard in the club house, that's why Attleborough had first class cricket and football teams. Of all the many people I have met in sport, Alfie has to be one of the best, a lovely man who will never be forgotten or replaced.

After Wembley its back to Wymondham and my first job was to sell programmes. That season Steve Cracknell and John Parry's team did so well to win promotion, they were all young lads mostly locals and as they grow older they will get better and become a good team. The club welcomed the Royal Navy Association to hold their meetings there and we appreciate their support. On their meeting days they have a fine buffet with a nice cheese selection and all are welcome to a glass of rum. After their meetings they all seem to sail home happy. Gemma and her ladies team also have started well, its good that the clubs have a ladies team. And thanks to Sharon our Delia Smith, her after match refreshments as many have said are the best in local football. Harvey with the help of Nigel do a good job in the club house and on match days Harvey's mates have their lunchtime drinks, of course Mossy has to be in charge. When Mossy came back from a holiday in Spain he did bring me some cheese, it was of a Barcelona flavour but it disappeared, Harvey must have eaten it or some big mice, the cheese was not the only thing to disappear as Ted Reynolds new underpants went missing from the dressing room. It seems that on match days Ted didn't wear his underpants as he can run faster without them. Also gone missing is a lad called Gonk who was going to do so much for the club, some say he has now moved to Norwich and is now a bus driver. If you see a bus coming down the road backwards it could be him.

I did attend the council meeting at the Central Hall, the place was packed it seemed all Wymondham had turned out to support the future of the Kings Head Meadow and like myself we all went home happy.

Thanks to Gemma and her ladies team who all came to give their support. Andy Gardiner spoke very well on behalf of his working party and it was agreed that the meadow will be kept green and a new lease would be offered to our football club. After a show of hands all were in agreement of the decision. It was pleasing that the large crowd gave Andy Gardiner and his working committee, also the rest of the council a round of applause in appreciation of the future of the King's Head Meadow.

Former Norwich City Players, Roger Hansbury & Duncan Forbes, still good friends with myself

Some members of Wymondham Sundays Team
Back left - right: Mike Musk (lines man), Les King (president), Kevin Piper, Derek Minns (chairman)
Front left - right: Nick Foyster, Tim Saunders (captain), Adie Lee

Former Norwich City Goal Keepers
Roger Hansbury, Mervyn Cawston, Sandy Kennon, Bryan Gunn

Tony Dickerson presents The Les King Trophy
to Wroxham player Shaun Wones

SMART SET: Wroxham Football Club first team players and officials face the camera before Saturday's opening Jewson League Premier Division match against Harwich at Trafford Park, which they won 6-0. They're pictured in front of the Les King Stand, newly named in honour of club life president Les King. Back (left to right): Damion Hilton, Shaun Cameron, Jason Fletcher, Russell Stock, Josh Carus, Stuart Parsons, John Edridge, Mark Fowler, Darren Terrington, Chris Wigger, Justin Fox, Peter Smith, Kenny Cooke and Les King. Front: Gavin Lemmon, Shaun Howes, Karl Horton, Darren Gill, Matty Neale, Craig Lewis, Paul Hartle and Paul Terrington.

A jubilant Wroxham manager Damian Hilton (back row, third left) and his assistant Greg Downs (second left) are joined by players and officials after clinching the Ridgeons League, Premier Division title at the weekend.

43

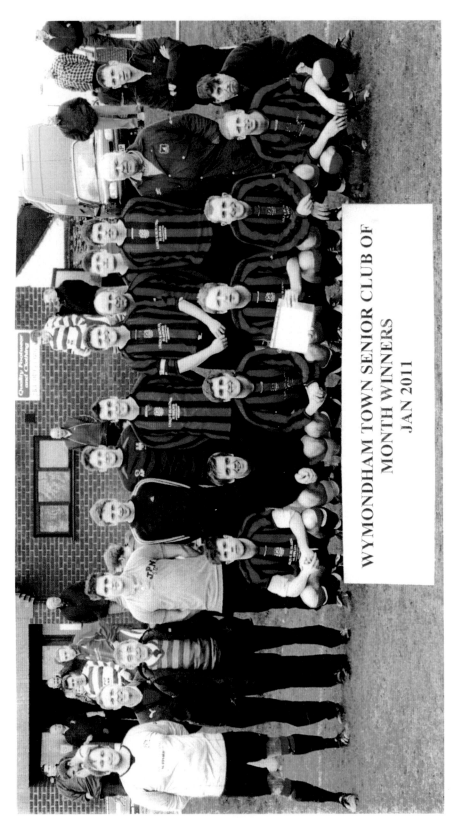

WYMONDHAM TOWN SENIOR CLUB OF MONTH WINNERS JAN 2011

LATEST YACHTSMEN: Wroxham FC's squad for the coming season. Back row (left to right): Tom Jarrett (chairman), Greg Downs (assistant manager), Gavin Pauling, Shaun Howes, Lee Howlett, Josh Carus, Graham Challen, Martyn Magee, Damian Hilton (player-manager), Kenny Cooke (treasurer), Pat Penn (chief executive), Tom Webster (general manager of Optic. Front, Les King (life president), Gavin Lemmon, Danny White, Lee Gilman, Justin Fox, Robert Woodcock, John Eldridge, Coren Hardy, Gary Gilmore, Tony Dickerson (deputy chairman).
Missing: Ben Carver, Dale Cooper, Andy Key, Ollie King and Ben Thompson.
Picture: SUPPLIE

45

Do you remember?

They were a handy team in their day... and a reunion was a great opportunity for the footballers to get back together again.

Big Les King, Mr Wymondham himself, was delighted when he turned up at the party for the former railway workers and bumped into his old mates.

"It was good to see them again. Being on the railway was like being part of a large family," said Les who went on to run a number of businesses after his railway days including the old Regal Cinema in Wymondham. Les met up with his chums at the annual reunion organised by Johnny Pipe at Arkwrights in Norwich which attracted more than 100 former workers from all over Norfolk and into Suffolk.

"Thanks to your stories the message got around and we had a brilliant reunion, probably the best yet," added Johnny.

The football team won the Thursday League three times running at one stage and in the picture we have: Arthur Nudds, Donny Goffin, Derek Peeke, Vic Crowe, Roy Collins, John Bellchamber, Bob Leeder and Les King.

Pat Penn, Julian Dicks, myself all happy at Wroxham FC

Bruce Cunningham, Kenny Cooke, Myself, Chris Green, Tony Dickerson

My friend Josh Carus receives the President's Trophy

Who do they support?

Two brothers and who do they support?

Wroxham League Champions again, with manager
Damien Hilton and Shaun Howes

Kenny Cooke on the gate at Wroxham

Wroxham Captain Stu Larter

Was this Wroxham's best ever team?

Dereham Town FC League Champions 2013

Maurice Graver, Maurice Stafford (Gentleman Footballer and Golfer) and myself

My mate Danny Wright from
Attleborough who has done so well in
professional football

Wroxham Manager David Batch's Team

In front of Les King stand is my mate Jack Hubbard, second from right front row

Dereham Town FC League Champions 2012 - 2013 season

52

CHAPTER 7

So this is Wembley

In the past much has been written of Wroxham FC, the Manchester United of local football. The club were league champions many times, and we went to Carrow Road and in seven visits, won the Norfolk Senior Cup five times, and the team won the treble in centenary year; I was with manager Bruce Cunningham and we had many happy years. No one will ever better Bruce's record in local football.

In 2009, David Batch became the manager at Wroxham, most of the players who were there stayed after new lads came and new manager David Batch's lads became the pride of local football when in 2010 they reached the final of the F.A. Vase to be played at the new Wembley Stadium.

First the team beat Gorleston 3-0 at home and then won 3-0 away at Northampton Spencer. Next was a 3-1 win at Halstead then the team were on their travels again as they won 3-1 at Flackwell Heath, next the team drew 1-1 away at Armthorpe Welfare, it was a draw at the replay at Wroxham but Wroxham won away 5-0 at Royston. Luck seemed against Wroxham as they were drawn away again at Needham Market and Wroxham once again upset the form book and won 2-1. After reaching the semi-final of the F.A. Vase the team would have to play White Hawk of division 1 of the Sussex County Football Leg. The team played at Brighton where Wroxham would have to play away in the first league. In the first leg, goals from Paul Cook, Andy Eastaugh saw Wroxham win 2-0. On Saturday April 3rd over 1200 people came to the second leg held at Wroxham. Colin Hazel and Kenny Cooke were on the gate and I sold over 1000 programmes, a club record. Wroxham got off to a great start as Steven Spriggs scored, five minutes later it was 2-0 as a great Shaun Howes free kick sailed into the net. At the end of the game, Wroxham had won 4-1 on aggregate and would play last seasons winners Whitley Bay at Wembley Stadium on Sunday May 9th 2010.

Now the hard work of ticket and travel arrangements had to be done. Who would get the VIP tickets and which hotel would the team stay in? Kenny Cooke, Colin Hazel, and Melly Arthurton spent many hours over time in the Dolphin office and Geoff Skeets was in charge of selling tickets at Wroxham. I was surprised as I sold over 100 tickets in Wymondham. There were two bus loads. Special thanks to Gary and Caroline Hubbard of the Anglian Sign Casting Company who had kindly supplied cast plaques to our opponents in the clubs great F.A Vase run. Later Colin Hazel and myself arranged from Mr and Mrs Hubbard a plaque for Kenny Cooke in recognition of all his hard work and support to Wroxham F.C. That plaque is now on the front of the club house.

Early on the Sunday morning, Wroxham Secretary Chris Green picked me up, we were on the way to Wembley. As the team were staying at a hotel in St Albans we stopped there for coffee and biscuits. We were given our tickets and the special Wembley match day programme. I was pleased as there was a two page write up on myself with the headline 'By Royal Appointment'. There was also a photo of myself with the Duke of Edinburgh when he dropped into Trafford Park in his helicopter. There was also a photo of Colin Hazel on the gate at Wroxham. When Wroxham lost 2-1 at Thamesmead Town, the gate was only 39, there are several teams in that league that didn't get 100 spectators for their home games. I would say that in Bruce Cunningham's day when we played Diss, Dereham, Sudbury, Lowestoft, and Wisbech there would be between 200 and 300 spectators watching those games. I can remember when Kenny Cooke, Colin Hazel and myself were on the gate and when we played Kings Lynn over 1200 spectators came, those days at Wroxham FC will never be beaten.

David Batch and his team did well to reach the F.A Vase final at Wembley. I can remember that two weeks before the game David Batch, myself and Captain Graham Challen, Vice Captain Martin McNeil went on the train to Wembley for final arrangement before the big game, I did take a picnic lunch and we found a quiet corner in the England dressing room to have our lunch.

On the final day, myself, Mr and Mrs Kenny Cooke, Mr and Mrs Colin Hazel and Secretary Chris Green sat for lunch where Royalty sit, the food was good with special lady waitresses service. I did have to tell Chris Green that this was Wembley and he could not ask for seconds. As I stood next to Kenny Cooke in the Royal Box, with Colin Hazel and saw all the hundreds that Kenny had arranged buses for to visit Wembley to support Wroxham, to me that was special and the best part of Wembley. The day had been great, we were all treated like royalty; you did not get too much to eat, however we did have a first class view from the Royal Box and many airliners passed overhead as they approached London Airport. I cannot write too much about the game as Wroxham lost 6-1 and Whitley Bay won the F.A. Vase for the second year running, but when you think that over 300 teams had been in the competition to start with, Wroxham had done so well to get to the final.

After the game, we were invited to the Bobby Moore lounge for food and drinks. We did not stay there for very long. As we made our way back to Wymondham we passed all the buses coming back to Norfolk. Many of us met for drinks in the Snooker club as the lager was much cheaper in Wymondham than Wembley.

By Royal Appointment

Wroxham president Les King hopes his Yachtsmen can be crowned champions at Wembley

⊳⊳ The King of Wembley.

Making a meal

Les King's getting used to Wembley, having become possibly the first person to have a picnic in the home team dressing room at the national stadium.

The Wroxham vice-president travelled down with a delegation manager Dave Batch, chairman Tom Jarrett, skipper Grabam Challen and fellow player Martin McNeill ahead of next month's FA Vase final.

Les took a pack-up for the journey. It was a hot day and there was a lot of walking to do. An inspection of the much criticised playing surface showed the recently-laid turf had bedded in, winning the seal of our approval from Les. The seats in the home dug-out were fine – especially Fabio Capello's.

But by the time Les and Co reached the home dressing room which Wroxham will use when they walk out to play Whitley Bay on May 9, it was time to eat. Out came the sausage rolls and the ham rolls and, while others looked on, Les, the manager and the chairman all tucked in.

"I was knackered by then," said Les. "I'd walked three miles and gone up 300 steps. I thought it was time to open the pack-up."

Hopefully next time he'll opening the champagne.

Tribute to Les much deserved

ANDY GARDINER, Norwich Road, Wymondham. Chris Lakey's April 10 article on Les King (pictured) was absolutely spot on.

If anybody deserves to have a special day at Wembley with his beloved Wroxham Football Club it's Les.

I am proud to say I have known Les all of my 48 years. Les has worked tirelessly for local sports clubs, organisations and charities. If Les was on a fund-raising assignment it was best to pay rather than receive a thick ear or a "how ar your ribs, bor".

Les always supported me in my county and tournament darts career when many, because I was difficult and controversial, turned their back. If I was wrong I had Les to answer to and that was not something I looked forward to.

Les was the same in my cricket career and was a good friend of Attleborough Cricket Club; he was also instrumental in the survival of his Hardingham Cricket Club in 1994, something that many have forgotten. I have enjoyed many fine times with Les King a hard, fair man and a great character of Wymondham and Norfolk. Enjoy your day, Les. You thoroughly deserve it.

Recently, I seem to have made a habit of bumping into Les King, who has associations with more sports clubs and organisation than anyone I have ever met. Les is a life President at Wroxham, where he has a stand named after him. Before Wroxham made it through their FA Vase semi-final, Les took nothing for granted: no touching the trophy, no thinking about Wembley, no talking about it. Now they're really and truly on their way, he becomes one of the best examples of a loyal follower and supporter of local football. I really hope he and thousands of others from East Anglia enjoy their big day out.

Wroxham FC Team Bus to Wembley with driver and navigator

A proud Mr & Mrs Tony Dickerson in the
Royal Box at Wembley

This lady went to Wembley as her son
played for Wroxham

Mr & Mrs Kenny Cooke with Mrs Linda Hazel at the special Wembley lunch

Myself and Colin Hazel also at the special Wembley lunch

Myself with Martin McNeil, Wroxham Vice Captain and Graham Challen, Captain

Myself with FA Vase Trophy at Wembley
which Wroxham did not win

Wroxham, in blue playing at Wembley

Left - right: David (Thatch) Ready, Clive Privett (Hedge), Gordon Little, Paul Gardiner

The little Monkey in the middle with minders at Wembley

Jason, Stiggy and Thatch don't look happy as Wroxham are losing

Wembley outing was fit for a King

He had a seat fit for a King – but after surveying Wroxham's humbling 6-1 FA Vase final defeat from the Royal Box at Wembley Les King insists the team's players can still hold their heads high.

"The players have got nothing to be ashamed of," said Les, 75, reflecting on the once-in-a-lifetime occasion.

"They are a great bunch of lads and they did their best. Over 500 teams entered the competition and they did well to get to the final. .

"Naturally when you get to Wembley you want to win the final but they didn't have any luck. The players were heartbroken afterwards but we are proud of them. What they have achieved will give the club a boost for next season and beyond."

He added: "Whitley Bay are the best side I have seen Wroxham play since they played Sudbury who got to Wembley over 20 years ago."

Club life president Les was one of a 20-strong Wroxham delegation sitting in the Royal Box who received VIP treatment and hospitality.

He was joined by Tony Dickerson, Paul Maxey, Malcolm Lemon, Peter Bugdale, Alan Royall, Geoff Skeets, Kenny Cooke, Martin Fryer, Colin Hazel, Tom Webster, Chris Green and their guests, who enjoyed a pre-match meal in the Wembley Suite.

"It was good that all these people who over the years have worked so hard for Wroxham enjoyed their special day out. The Wembley officials made us all very welcome and the hospitality was first class.

"We were all privileged to be sitting in the Royal Box. At half time everybody else went to get refreshments but I just stood there and took in the whole occasion and looked around to see how many people I knew.

"You can get a drink or a bite to eat at any time but how many chances do you get to stand at Wembley at half time? I just wanted to look around to see all the people who had made the effort."

Les said the fact that Wroxham will never play in a Vase final at Wembley again, because future finals will be held elsewhere, made the occasion even more special.

"We heard it was the last FA Vase final to be held at Wembley so it was great that we got there in time. It was the icing on the cake for me."

Great day out: Les King salutes the fans from the Wembley Royal Box at half time, and below, enjoys the hospitality with, from left: Linda Hazel, Connie Cooke, Kenny Cooke (treasurer) and Chris Green (secretary)

Field of dreams: Wembley Stadium. Photo PA

Cheer leader: Les King, second left, joins the team to celebrate Wroxham's 2-1 win over Whitehawk. Photo: Nick Butcher

At the age of 75, Norfolk's "King of Sport" thought he had seen it all.

But now the irrepressible Les King is gearing up to write another new chapter in his well-documented sporting life after watching his beloved Wroxham book their place at Wembley.

One of the most familiar faces on the local sporting scene is looking forward to adding his distinctive voice to the Wembley roar when the Yachtsmen emerge from the tunnel on May 9 to face FA Vase holders Whitley Bay.

"I am 75 years old and when you get to that age this is like the icing on the cake.

"It's something I thought I would never live to see," said Les, who is Wroxham life president and even has the main stand named after him at the Trafford Park ground.

"I am so pleased about it. I haven't really even thought about winning the FA Vase. For me the main thing was getting there."

He added: "I am so pleased that people like Kenny Cooke, Tony Dickerson, Alan Royall and Patt Penn will be getting some reward for all the hard work they have put into the club over the years.

"There are probably about eight people who have been there for over 25 years and have stuck together through thick and thin. I don't think there are too many clubs around like that."

During his tenure Les has banged the drum for the Yachtsmen at every available opportunity – a cheer-leader in chief for all seasons.

Speak to him about anything and you can bank on him mentioning his Wroxham life presidency at some point, usually quite early in the conversation.

Over the years he's had plenty to shout about as honours arrived on a conveyor belt at Trafford Park during the Bruce Cunningham era. Since 1992 seven Eastern Counties League Premier Division championship triumphs and seven Norfolk Senior Cups helped to turn the Yachtsmen into the most dominant force in local football. There were other trophies aplenty. But curiously they struggled to make a major impact in

the FA Vase – until now. Ironically during one of the most barren periods for silverware in the club's history. Les believes that good old-fashioned teamwork has been the key. "We have got the best keeper around in Scott Howie and we have had a certain amount of luck, which you need in football," said Les.

"This team is probably not the best side Wroxham have ever had over the years but the players all work so hard for each other and you have got to give credit to the manager David Batch and his assistants.

"The lads all play for one another and as the season has gone on they have got better as a team – they are

on the same wavelength.

"I go into the dressing room and help with the team talks. I have always been made welcome by the managers. I always give people support and encouragement and if somebody isn't doing very well I still give them encouragement."

Les, who worked on the gate on Saturday as over 1,200 filed through to watch the 2-1 (4-1 agg) win over Whitehawk, hopes the Vase run can be the catalyst for a fan base boost.

"Hopefully now we have got to Wembley we'll be able to get more people through the gate for our games now they have seen what a good team Wroxham are."

> 'There are probably about eight people who have been there for over 25 years and stuck together through thick and thin. I don't think there are too many clubs like that'
>
> LES KING, WROXHAM LIFE PRESIDENT

From Welfare to Wembley

Alzheimer's Society — Leading the fight against dementia

Sponsored by Design Ltd

Brian Totty Ski

CHAPTER 8

Cricket

I have written about local cricket in my past books but as this year's local cricket season has just finished, I can now bring you up to date. The weather in March and April had been wet and cold with my president charity game due to be played on Sunday April 21st. I became worried and hoped that the weather would get better. Hardingham groundsman Dale Watson said that he would do his best to get the wicket ready. On Saturday, the day before the game, as if by miracle the rain stopped and the sun came out. The Sunday was a lovely hot day, in fact it was the start of a long summer, the best for many years, some days when watching cricket it was best not to sit in the sun as it was very hot.

Not only was the weather good, the cricket was also good with local teams doing very well, my club Hardingham had a very good season with the Saturdays team doing well.

 The first team won their league, the second team came third in their league and the third team also won their league. This was the first season of new chairman Dale Watson. The club also have two Sunday teams and this season a score of 403 from 40 overs was the highest ever scored by a Hardingham team.

Over the years we have talked of Andy Gardiner, when Andy hit a six the ball would go high over the trees in the big wood opposite, but more recently another Andy, Andy Duckham joined the club and he has hit the ball just as high and hard for his sixes as Andy Gardiner did. Andy Duckham scores even more runs when his mum arrives in her camper van.

Over the years Hardingham have had some good teams, Dick Flatt's side won the League five years running. Years later, Andy Gardiner's team did well and this season Hardingham's first team won their league.

Another club where I like to visit is Great Witchingham, there are some good lads there and Paul Rogers and his family always make you welcome. I can remember when Sam Artherton was a young lad, he wanted to become a boxer, I told him to stick with cricket, now Sam is one of Norfolk's best ever cricketers and also plays for Essex. There are also some good young lads at the club and it was pleasing for many people when Great Witchingham beat Vauxhall Mallards to win the Carter Cup.

I have been watching cricket at Swardeston for many years now, from the days of the village team to the champions of East Anglian Premier League. I think the club's best achievement was when they won the Cockspur National 20-20 cup at the Rose Bowl at Southampton in 2010. This was on Sky TV and I can remember when we all sat down at the Snooker club all day and watched how well Swardeston played, a team of lads from just down the road were watched by people all over the country, this had to be special. This season Swardeston have again won the East Anglian Premier League for the second year running. Over the years I have wrote of many good players and clubmen at Swardeston, but one man who has to be mentioned is the most hard working man I have met in cricket, and is my friend Pat Hall.

I also like to go and watch cricket at Horsford where you can sit and watch the planes coming in to land. I think with the good weather here this summer instead of travelling on the holiday jets I could be sitting watching cricket at Horsford. At lunch another hard working man in cricket is Colin Crisp who goes to the local fish and chip shop and brings chips back to go with your cheese sandwiches. When at Horsford you will always see President Marcus Wilkinson there, Marcus was very good at football and cricket in his Younger days, now when you see him he is always on the march with his pint of lager and his regiment marching behind, its good as they support local sport and they deserve a pint.

It was good to see on TV and in the local press the hard working ladies of Rocklands Cricket Club who won the Best Tea in Cricket award. I have been there and did a Cup Final presentation and the food was very good. I think Hethersett and Tas Valley club would come a close second as not only is it a great place to watch cricket but at tea if you support the home or away team you are invited to have a cup of tea and cakes.

England did beat Australia to retain the Ashes, I did not like this D.R.S. system it did not do Australia any favours, I think its best to stick with the two umpires as it has always been. They did go home with some credit as they won the one day series to get their revenge. I think it could be different next time in Australia.

After much hard work by all at the Hardingham Club including the Fowle family and Chairman Andrew Falcon, new changing rooms and showers were built, myself and England cricketer Matthew Fleming did the official opening in 2010. That year our Sunday side won the Peter Parfitt League and he came and presented the trophy.

Swardeston Cricket Team, winners of The Cockspur Cup at The Rose Bowl, Southampton

Back row left - right: Daniel Martin, James Pearson, Will Rist, Michael Eccles, Peter Thomas, Sam Thelwell, Peter Lambert, Jonny Cooper, Norman Bygrave. *Front row left - right:* Ed Hopkins, George Walker, Mark Thomas, Jaden Hatwell, Ian Tufts, Richard Sims

A very good Great Witchingham Team

■ Carter Cup winners Great
Witchingham: Back row – Sam Groves,
Stephan Joubert, Will Dunger, James
Page, Shaun Arthurton, Carl Rogers.
Front row – James Hale, James Spelman,
Sam Arthurton, Tom Collishaw (captain),
Jonathan Spelman, Kieran Bunting.

Hardingham are on the up

HARDINGHAM life president Les King has paid tribute to "heavyweight partner" Andy Gardiner for sparking a revival at the ailing club.

The outlook looked bleak when Hardingham, Norfolk League Division One champions in 1984, slumped into Division Six last season, but the arrival of the league's record-breaking batsman Gardiner has heralded an upturn, which sees them back in the promotion running.

And King this week heaped praise on the man who for over a decade was the driving force behind Attleborough's rise from pub team to Division Three outfit.

"I am very pleased with the way things have been changed around. The first team are doing well, there is a good spirit in the

DOUBLE ACT: Hardingham duo Les King and Andy Gardiner.

● ● ● ● ● ● ●

A team captained by David Young and we've got a lot of youngsters coming through.

"Andy and me get on quite well because we are both heavyweights – we stick together." quipped Les

Taking cover

Norfolk are left waiting in the rain

Page 31

Hardingham Cricket Club after winning the Peter Parfitt League

CHAPTER 9

Sport for all

Over the past two years it's been great for British sport. First team GB, heroes of London 2012, Britain's golden games, the best Olympics ever.

You have read many times of our great athletes, and the great wins for our teams. Twenty-nine golds, seventeen silver and nineteen bronze, our best ever.

There are many moments in sport that make you feel happy, first I must write when the Queen's horse 'Estimate' won the gold cup at Ascot. The Queen, a great lady was so happy and pleased that her horse had won.

After Mo Farah won his 2 gold medals in the Olympics, his little daughter, Rhianna, ran to the track, she was so proud of her dad and they all joined in the Mo bot dance. Then we had the great Usain Bolt, after his last race just recently which he won he was given a bunch of flowers, after the race he gave the flowers to a little girl. She was so happy he stayed with her and signed so many autographs. Usain Bolt has always said he would like to be like the great Mohammad Ali, well I think he is – I rate him the best athlete ever. But my favourite of all is Christine Ohurougu, the 400 metres world champion. She is so happy when she wins.

More recently I watched the Great North Run on TV, it was a great four hour programme and with three great runners, Mo Farah, Kenenisa Bekele and Haile Gebrselassie leading the race, they seemed to be running as fast as the Red Arrows flying overhead. After running 13 miles these three great athletes all shook hands smiling and not even sweating, they all signed autographs for many, as they looked so fit you would have thought they had just had a walk in the park.

It is a pity all these highly paid footballers don't have time for the public who support them. I have seen some walk by youngsters as if they are not there. They should follow our athletes and rugby players who have time for all who support them. All these rugby players are big lads, they do not earn much money, but when they go out and have a few beers they do know how to behave.

When I was driving by the Rec on Browick Road, where so many football teams used to play, football there has now gone and credit must be given to Wymondham Rugby Club who now play at the Rec, and so many youngsters are encouraged to play rugby. There are also some good lads in local sport. First I must write of my friend Ashley Watson, not only is he a first class cricketer, he's a brave member of our armed forces. Ashley has served in Iraq and several times in Afghanistan. I have seen him score a century for Norfolk, also a century in my charity game at Hardingham. Then there's my mate Clive

Privett 'hedge' who sets a fine example to play sport as you grow old. At 66 years old Clive still plays tennis, football and cricket and if you listen to him he always wins. Another good lad who enjoys sport is my mate Nathan Gostling, when he was a young lad he won the Norfolk School Boy Championship at squash, later playing football and cricket at Mattishall, win or lose he's happy and is a top lad for Fitness Express. Then there is my mate Aaron Johnson, this lad doesn't seem to have the best of luck, he is very keen with his five-a-side team playing at Goal at the Hewett School where many young lads enjoy their football. If you listen to Aaron his team always wins. Aaron did win the Fitness express golf day and like Nathan, he is also a top lad at Fitness Express.

There are now many clubs in football, cricket, boxing, to help youngsters to take up sport. This they should support as when I was young I played football, cricket and was a boxer, (not very good). In 1977 I won the Culyer first squash trophy at Barnham Broom and in 1983 became the club's first tennis champion. I later and still am a life member of the golf club and won the first shareholder's trophy.

These days I swim at Park Farm and for the past three years I have won the 10 mile title. It's easy for me as with my weight I can float and if you have time you can swim all day. When you leave school and take up sport, join a fitness club and you will have more enjoyment and save money.

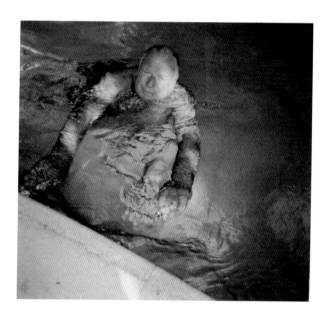

Park Farm Swimming Champion 2008

Top man, Ashley Watson

A happy sportsman, Nathan Gostling

Three good lads of Norfolk Cricket: George Walker, Mark Thomas, Tim Sheppard

Aaron Johnson, Park Farms,
1st Golf Trophy winner

A happy trio, Michael Betts,
Mac Gardiner, Ken Brown

Barnham Broom Junior Golf team when sponsored by myself

Boxing Champions Frances Ampofo, Colin McMillan with MC Danny Maloney

Sport and wildlife on display in my office

Three good friends, Dave Stringer,
Neil Sturman, former Norfolk Heavyweight Champion and Ken Brown

Two Golf Pros Joe Miller and Andrew Marshall

Having a Friday night drink, Rob Scarl, Danny Nobbs, TV Brian Hawes, Clive Privett Hedge

CHAPTER 10

Enjoy sport and help local charities

There are many people who take part, and play in sports teams and they also help local charities. I am Life President of the Wymondham and Attleborough Charity Darts League. I had sponsored this league for ten years. Each year I go and present the trophies to the winners and each year this darts league gives £2,000 to local charities. They have been good to my charities, Star Throwers and Chapel Road School.

My mate, boxer Jackson Williams I sponsored when he started boxing, went to America and ran across America like Forrest Gump. He ran and ran and ran and raised thousands for his local charity.

Recently Radio Norfolk sports reporter Nick Bowler did a sponsored parachute jump. I saw Nick recently at a cricket match and he told me it was a great experience jumping out of an aeroplane and he raised over £1100 for his local charity. I did tell Nick it would be better if he could get on Saturday's shows more local football reports and results, than having to listen to the Norwich City phone-ins on Radio Norfolk.

Another lad who deserves credit is former heavyweight boxing champion Sam Sexton. Sam who now owns KO Sports Diner in Norwich has made Star Throwers his charity and when I had my film show at the old Regal for Help for Heroes, Sam came with other boxers.

Norfolk builder Chris Brown flew half way across the world and cycled 3,483 miles from Los Angeles to Boston to raise money in memory of his beloved wife Sharon. Chris and his wife Sharon enjoyed cycling and in 2001 they cycled on a tandem recumbent bike to Gretna Green where they got married. Chris Brown's cycle ride across America raised £5,500 for Star Throwers who gave his Sharon hope.

Another special young lady Emily Parr, cycled over 500 miles across Mexico in 2006 and raised £3,800 for cancer charity Macmillan. In recent years Emily has been a great help to Star Throwers and now she is happy and busy in their charity shop.

There are many more people who enjoy sport and raise money for their charities.

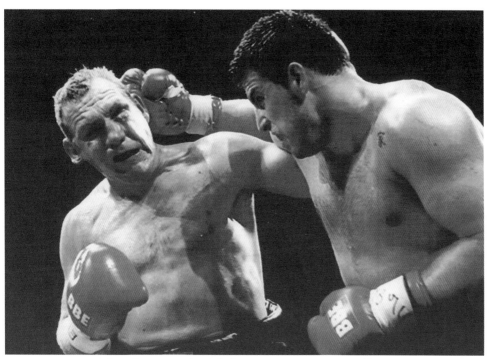

Sam Sexton on the right beats Martin Rogon in Belfast
to win the Commonwealth Heavyweight Title

Myself presenting a trophy to ladies winning darts team.
Shaz Eglan, Barbara Palmer, Nikki Goldsmith, Jane Goldsmith

Some people who have supported my charity events

Mark Wilkinson presents a cheque to
Wendy Winterbottom

Kenny Cooke and Mick Money

Stephen and Andy Culyer with
Ivan (Shorty) Stubbings

Hop, Lewis, Shorty, Luke and Daniel, all happy

My wife Anita with her friend Leigh Smith

Myself with John Smith

THANKS to Colin Hazel of Hazel Butchers & David Smith of Hi-Span

CHAPTER 11

Chapel Road School
For children with special needs

I can remember early in 1986 having a drink in the Ex-Serviceman's Club on a Saturday evening with Bernard Daynes and his wife, Alan Buster Farrow and Ray Willis. Bernard whose son Matthew was a pupil at Chapel Road School, asked if we could do a charity event for the School, my mate Buster suggested we could be like Ian Botham and walk from London to Wymondham. I replied that when I have had a few drinks, I have a job to walk home, but within five minutes Stuart Perkins, Bob Howes and Barney Howes said that they would give us £100 each if we could walk from London and Ray Willis who worked for me said that he would be the backup driver.

The next day, I spoke to my friend Peter Steward who worked for the local press, he said that he would walk with us and get us bright jackets to wear. After two months of training, myself, Buster Farrow, Bernard Daynes and Peter Steward walked from London. £3000 was raised from the walk, the best charity event for the school so far.

A few days later the headmaster Phil Thomas wrote to me and asked if I would consider becoming Chairman of the Friends, this according to the rules a one year position. I did visit the school and the headmaster took me to the classrooms and I met the children, teachers and volunteers, they all worked so hard caring for the children. After that visit, it was the best that I could do to become chairman.

After one year headmaster Phil Thomas said that if the rules could be changed would I stay as Chairman of the Friends as the past year had been the schools best fundraising year. Now 27 or 28 years later, I am still the chairman, with me all these years is our treasurer John Goode a former bank manager, he looks after the money. We have also had a special hard working little lady Gloria Myers, our secretary for many years. We have been lucky as for many years now we have had so many hard working committees and all of our team care for the children. There are also many kind people who have helped the School with fund raising events.

I can remember after opening the fete at the Wayland hospital I asked headmaster Phil Thomas if our school could have a fete this year. This has been done for many years now and thanks to our hard working committee over £2000 was raised, the best yet. The past two years I have invited the Attleborough Lady Mayors, Karen Pettitt and Samantha Taylor to be our guests, I seem to get on well with Lady Mayors.

Recently it was suggested that it would now be possible to have film shows at the school for the children. Many years ago when I ran the Regal Cinema in Wymondham and the film that was showing was something like Jungle Book I asked Joe Smith who kept a bus opposite the cinema if he would pick the children up from the school and bring them to the cinema – this he did free of charge. The children loved the films and I made sure that they all had a bag of sweets and an ice cream. Years ago at Christmas, we would have a Christmas lunch and I would be Father Christmas and give all the children their presents. It seemed I was the right size to be Father Christmas. All of the Father Christmases seem to be big lads, I often wonder how they get down chimneys.

After Phil Thomas retired, the school had a new head teacher. This lady was Karin Heap and she was happy to join our committee. I did arrange charity football and cricket games for the school and I suggested that the school should have our own Olympics day. This was a great event and champion boxer Jon Thaxton came as a guest, the weather was good and the children all joined in and enjoyed this good fund raising event. Later, footballer Robert Fleck visited the school and I joined in a few events. In 2006 myself and my friend Karen Scriven who worked at Park Farm did a six mile sponsored walk through Thetford Forest, it was on a hot day, I did ask Karen if we could sit down and have a rest but the answer was no, if we stop we might not start again, well we were in the middle of Thetford Forest, once again no score but we did raise £550 for the school.

Some mornings at the school assembly people who have done fundraising are invited to join in with the children and staff after the visit they go away pleased at how well the school is run and are happy that they have given their support. Over the past few years the school seems to get more and more busy. Our head teacher and the school governors are working hard, hopefully one day we could have a new school and recently MP George Freeman and the Minister of Education Michael Gove came to visit. The school's assistant Head Teacher, Dylan Yates and his helpers are now working hard to get the school's charity shop open before the end of the year. It would be good for me if my two charities could both have a charity shop, Star Throwers in Wymondham and our school in Attleborough, that would help to keep me busy. Over the years many kind people have served on our committee, some have now left and are no longer with us but they will always be remembered for their hard work and kindness to the children.

Committee member Andrea with her
two lads James and Jason

Our hard working secretary for many years
Gloria Myers

Barbara Palmer presenting a cheque raised at
Wymondham Snooker Club

Mrs Brenda Ford (Lady Mayor) welcomes the
London walkers back, Bernard Daynes,
Alan Farrow, Peter Steward, Les King

Myself with Treasurer John Goode
about to open a new play area

Myself with Karen Scriven in Thetford Forest
on our sponsored walk

Long serving members of The Friends of Chapel Road School:
Sue Knowles Savage, Anita Clements, Les King, Ida Thorpe

The delivery of the school's new bus from the variety club, with guests on back row:
Dennis McAvoy from Dunston Hall, Myself, Treasurer John Goode, TV Star Trisha and
bus driver John Kirk with happy children all wanting a ride in the new bus.

CHAPTER 12

Help for Heroes

My Friend Arthur Nudds was the gamekeeper for Sir Richard and Lady Dannatt who lived at Keswick Mill. Sir Richard Dannatt was at the time the head of the British Army. Arthur arranged for me to meet Sir Richard, and when I met him I stood to attention and saluted. He asked of my army days and I reported that I was Private King and served in Korea.

I was asked if I could help his charity, Help for Heroes, and I agreed to hold a film show and was promoted to Sergeant. The next day I spoke to Michael Armstrong, he said he would ask the Ex Servicemen's Club if we could use the old cinema which they kindly agreed to. The film that I wanted to show was the Memphis Belle. Years ago when I showed this film I made cinema history as I knew the pilot of the Flying Fortress B17 and he flew the Memphis Belle over the cinema and did a fly past over Wymondham. Trevor Wickes of Hollywood Cinema kindly supplied the film.

The day was set for Sunday August 9th 2009 at 2.30pm. I invited as guests, Norwich City legend Duncan Forbes and boxers Jon Thaxton, Sam Sexton, Danny McIntosh, Corporal Archer of the Light Dragoons, Corporal Gallagher from the Parachute Regiment and Lloyd Frosdick from the Royal Marines, and they all came.

On Friday before the film show I arranged for Wroxham to come and play Wymondham Town for my Presidents Trophy as I am Life President of both clubs. About 300 watched the game, which was won by Wroxham, and they kindly supported the raffle to help the film show takings.

On the Sunday the cinema was full and when the soldiers came in they got a standing ovation. I would like to thank all of the kind people who donated raffle prizes and bought cinema tickets. It was good for me to return to the cinema for that afternoon, this was the first charity event held locally for Help for Heroes and £2,750 was raised.

When Sir Richard Dannatt heard of that he was so pleased he agreed to come and meet myself and Michael Armstrong. On Thursday August 20th Sir Richard and Lady Dannatt came to Park Farm, Hethersett, I presented Sir Richard with the cheque, he kindly gave me a signed book of his Regiment, The Green Howards, the lunch was kindly provided by Park Farm and the flowers for Lady Dannatt were provided by Dawn from The Flower Shed.

I did receive a letter from Sir Richard at the Ministry of Defence and he said thank you and the people of Wymondham who really do care about the Armed Forces on the front line in Afghanistan and previously in Iraq.

A few weeks after the film show myself, my wife Anita and Michael Armstong and gamekeeper Arthur were all invited to lunch at Keswick Mill and Lady Dannett did the cooking. When Sir Richard retired from the Army I was invited to the last shoot of the season and a special lunch at Keswick, and I have now moved up to Captain King and myself and Arthur could be in line for the minders job for the now *Lord* Dannatt . . .

Sir Richard and Lady Phillipa Dannatt visit Park Farm to receive a cheque for £2750 from Les King and Michael Armstrong in support for Help for Heroes

Sir Richard with his two minders

Film Showing

Our Special Guests at the Film Show

Michael Armstrong, myself, my wife Anita, Sir Richard & Lady Dannatt, Arthur Nudds

Boxers, Sam Sexton, Jon Thaxton, Danny McIntosh

Stan Kelly and Roy Plackett presenting me with a painting of the Memphis Belle

My friend Roy Plackett buys 4 choc bars from this special ice cream lady, Leigh Smith

Joan Parry who kindly sold raffle tickets at my film and charity football games

The following 3 pages of pictures are from my scrapbook

Myself with my mate Nudds, I think he's had too much to drink

My Mum and Dad in their younger days, don't they look smart. They will never be forgotten.

I could not write a book and forget my right hand man for 40 years, NEIL

Doreen looks happy with her friend Stiggy

Myself and Simon Caston with my Dad's steam engine at the Show Ground

With my mate Buzzer, I have never met a man who eats as much as him

Ralph Firman Snr, myself and racing drivers Ralph Firman Jnr and Martin Donnelly at Ralph's birthday celebrations at The Stag, Attleborough

Myself and Jon Thaxton lead the way to promote Kelling Heath Holiday Camp and Leisure Centre

PREPARATION: Mark Wilkinson *Left - right:* Amy Greenwood, Mick Mason, Les King, Dylan Yates, Alex Brake and Kate Brewster with Dalton at the launch of the Scrappage Rally at the Bird in Hand pub in Wreningham

Name your top ten: The other day I had the pleasure of meeting Les King, who was voted the most well-known person in Wymondham since Robert Kett by listeners of Radio Norfolk.

Les was guest of honour at the opening of estate agency Money and Duncan's new premises in Market Street.

I asked Les why he thought he had received so many votes and how he felt about such a compliment.

"More people know me than Robert Kett, but he got hung! They know me because I ran the Regal Cinema for 30 years, I have sponsored a lot of local sport and I'm chairman, president, vice-president and life president of many sports clubs – boxing, football and cricket. I'm also chairman of the Friends of Chapel Road School in Attleborough for children with special needs. This is the repayment for things I have done over the years – a sort of recognition," he said.

Man of Wymondham: Les King has been granted a distinguished accolade – and been interviewed by Mercury columnist Jenny Francis

Committee member Steve Taylor with his daughters Amy and Lucy at the School Fete

Anita Clements, a former Miss Wymondham, a great help to me at Chapel Road

CHAPTER 13

Days out

THE ROYAL NORFOLK SHOW

My mate Arthur Nudds rang me one evening in early June and said that Sir Richard was going to be the President of the Royal Norfolk Show and would we like to go as his guests. Arthur said Prince Harry was coming as one of Sir Richard's guests. I replied if Prince Harry was going we should also go.

On the show day Arthur came to mine and off we went by taxi and went to the main King George entrance, there was a queue but there was also an entrance for guests, so we went straight in.

We visited most of the wild life stands and made our way to the grand ring and when we went up the steps to the seating area the attendant said we were in the wrong place, special guests only. Arthur said "we are guests" we were then shown to our seats. There were show judges and many posh people with bowler hats and badges, we did get some strange looks as people must have thought we were in the wrong place, but we did get a good view of the events.

Next we made our way to the Presidents Pavilion for lunch, as we entered the man in charge asked if we were in the right place, once again there were many people in bowler hats and badges, some I would call Hooray Henrys. I don't like people who think they are better than others. At that moment just as I was going to tell the man in charge we were guests, Sir Richard and Lady Dannett arrived and we joined them for lunch, we were two old country boys but we were treated like Royalty. Later in the afternoon we went in the Farmers Union tent where we were served with tea and sandwiches, they must have thought we were land owners or farmers. Late afternoon our taxi picked us up, the only money we spent that day was the taxi fare.

Our day out at the show did prove, if you do good things to help others, you do get well treated.

Myself and Arthur with Butch and Linda Caddy

Prince Harry enjoying his day

A view of the hounds from the Grand Ring

Arthur with Sir Richard and Lady Dannett

MID NORFOLK RAILWAY

After our visit to the Royal Norfolk Show myself and my mate Arthur went on another journey from Dereham to Wymondham as guests of the Mid Norfolk Railway. As myself and Arthur worked in the loco at Dereham on the Railway, I was the driver and Arthur my fireman, each year many who worked locally on the Railway are invited for a train trip to Wymondham Abbey and return.

We would all meet at Dereham Station, tea and refreshments were offered on our arrival. We all met outside at the front of the station for a group photo then we board the train for our reserved seats, first stop is Yaxham then the ladies serve tea and sandwiches, just like the main line train. Next stop Thuxton then we pass through Hardingham, we look across the fields looking for hares and deer. Next we stop at Kimberley and a few yards from the platform is the house where I used to live and I look at the bedroom where I had my first honeymoon when I married my first wife Sylvia. In them days, you had to wait until you were married before you had a honeymoon. I shall always remember that bedroom at Kimberley Park.

When we arrived at Wymondham, our engine ran around the train in the old Briton Brush siding where I used to work when I left school and on our return trip to Dereham we are once again served with refreshments. When we leave Wymondham, on our left are the many allotments, where most grow vegetables but I know someone who seems to grow nettles and weeds. Next we cross the bridge at Crownthorpe, and when we get back to Dereham we are once again made welcome for refreshments. On the Mid Norfolk Railway there are many volunteers who work hard, there is always so much maintenance to keep the trains running but as the years go by the Mid Norfolk Railway gets better and many enjoy the train trips, like myself you can catch the train to Dereham and shop at Morrisons which is only 50 yards from the station and its cheaper by train than it is to drive there.

Mayflower steam train at Dereham

Mayflower steam train arrives at
Wymondham Abbey

Mayflower steam train leaving
Wymondham Abbey

New steam train Tornado passing my bungalow

A tanker steam train about to cross
Crownthorpe bridge

70013 Britannia Class leaving
Wymondham for Cambridge

BUS TRAVEL TO NORWICH

I think it is good that when you retire from work you can get a free bus pass, it helps many people, less traffic on the road, no car parking and helps people to keep more active with their days out. It also helps the shops in Wymondham as people come from Hethersett and Attleborough on the bus.

After having a swim I catch the bus to Norwich at Hethersett where my lad Ian lives. Most days when I am at the bus stop there's a nice little lady on her way to meet her friend in Norwich for their weekly days out, some days they go to Yarmouth Market or Dereham for lunch and shopping. I have heard a lady moan if a bus is a few minutes late, she was going to report the driver. I told her if she did that they should take her bus pass away then she can walk, she has not spoke to me since.

I get off the bus in St Stephens and I like Iceland and Poundland for my shopping, then I walk to Norwich market and visit Joe's pets to see my mate Joe Sylvester, if you take your dog there the dog can try before you buy. Joe's son in law is my mate Damian Hilton, Damian used to play for Wroxham then became manager and his team won the League and Senior Cup at Carrow Road. Damian is now doing well as Manager of Norwich United.

Next it's Reggie's food stall which is run by Richard Lovett, for coffee and pies. Richard was a good boxer and boxed for my Lads Club, there is also a mushy pea stall and I do like a bag of chips. If you wish you can have a Chinese from I think it's called Chink Changs. I next see my mate Alex Pond at his flower stall, Alex is a keen fisherman and tells me about all the fish he catches at Kimberley Hall.

Before I leave the Market I call at the fruit stall which is run by Jon Thaxton's brother Jason for an update boxing report. Next comes the hardest job as we sit on the walk opposite Primark and people watch. There are many people walking past that I know and some days there is a good country and western singer and you can sit and listen to him sing for hours. If the weather is not good you can walk to Castle Meadow and catch a bus to Thorpe Station where you can sit and watch the trains arrive and depart. Then we catch the bus and make our way home. Like myself there are many people who enjoy their days out, thanks to the bus pass and bus companies.

Sean King, Mrs Caroline Hubbard and myself, people watching at the Walk

Joe Sylvester of Joes Pets

Richard Lovett, Go Go and myself at
Reggies Refreshment

Jason, Chris Scott and myself at
Jason's Fruit Stall

New steam train Tornado arrives at
Norwich Station

CHAPTER 14

The Queen's Diamond Jubilee

On Saturday June 2nd 2012 Wymondham was packed with thousands of local people who enjoyed the sunshine as the streets were packed for the town's Diamond Jubilee celebrations.

Weeks before the event was to take place Daniel Cox and his hard working committee invited me to be King of Wymondham for the day and the Queen for the day would be Violet May Royal. I thought this was a good choice as for years Violet pushed Alfie Royal everywhere in his wheelchair. Alfie helped many in Wymondham and local football.

The parade started from Back Lane. The Smokehouse Blue marching jazz band and myself and Violet led the procession in a classic car. The streets were packed, there were fancy dress competitions, hundreds of children enjoyed a party lunch. There was a beer festival at the Green Dragon. Daniel Cox who helped to organise said he was keen to pass the credit for the huge success of the day to the many town clubs and shops that took part.

I did write a letter that was in the local press thanking Daniel Cox for kindly inviting me to be King of Wymondham for this special day to celebrate the Queen's 60 year reign and to celebrate all that's good in Wymondham.

I was honoured to make the speech which welcomed people on such a special day. There were thousands of people, the most I have ever seen and at the end of my speech there were cheers and applause when all agreed that the Queen would be our Queen for many years to come.

I wrote in my letter that it was a credit to all who worked so hard to make this a happy day that Wymondham will never forget. A big thank you to all of them on behalf of Wymondham.

KING AND QUEEN: Royalty at the Wymondham Jubilee Procession, Les King & Violet May Royall

Young children looking forward to the
Fancy Dress Competition

Daniel Cox introduces myself to welcome
people to Wymondham

Kerrie Smy and Emma Williams who helped to promote Star Throwers Charity Shop

Mrs Gill Whall and Mrs Anne Steward, two hard working ladies who have helped many people

CHAPTER 15

Regal Re-Run

When I was about 17, I would cycle from Hingham and play football for Fred Hall's Wymondham Town team at the King's Head Meadow. At that time I had a girlfriend who lived at Wicklewood and we would both cycle to the Regal Cinema, we would sit on the back row but it was holding hands only.

In 1957 I boxed the great Ginger Sadd over four rounds. We were top of the billing at the Women's Institute which used to be on Vimy Ridge. A few months later I beat Ray Bracy from Dereham, this was the last boxing show held in Wymondham.

When I lived at Kimberley Station with my first wife Sylvia, we would cycle, with her sitting behind me, to the Women's Institute Hall where I was a doorman/bouncer, where I had previously boxed. It was the days of Kenny Ball and Acker Bilk and many other jazz bands who had played there. I was paid ten shillings for my work but it was harder work cycling home with Sylvia on the back of the bike than throwing out someone from the dance hall who had caused trouble. This was the time when trucks full of RAF personnel from RAF Watton would come to the Dance Hall, so I was always kept busy but nothing that I could not deal with.

In 1965 when I was married to my second wife Valerie, we had two little boys, Ian, who was named after Ian St John who scored the winning goal for Liverpool at Wembley and Sean, who was named after Sean Connery.

In 1965 there was an advert in the local press, looking for a man who could maintain strict discipline at the Regal Cinema in Wymondham. A friend of mine Cliffy Laskey went and met Roy Dashwood and told him there was a 'rough old boy' living at Hingham who could 'do the job'. Colin Dashwood came to see me and again I went on my bicycle to the Regal and the rest is now history.

In 1966 when England won the World Cup I became manager and worked for Roy Dashwood for 14 years, his longest ever employee. I worked at his Washington Night Club, the first of its kind in Norwich, many top stars appeared there as well as there being strip show nights and gambling evenings. I was there for seven years and there was very rarely any trouble or anything that I could not sort out.

I was at the Regal Cinema for about thirty years. I employed a lot of good people and many paid their respects when I held my charity event 'The Regal Reunion' recently.

When I was at the Regal I also had a butchers meat stall on the Wymondham Market. I employed a good butcher called Joe Austin and we would sell out by midday.

When I ran Olympic Removals and Freight Delivery Service, we moved all of the Norwich City footballers.

I bought my sports shop from my friend John Culyer about 25 years ago and when I left the Regal Cinema it was renamed King of Sport and I then became a shop keeper. The shop did really well but when parts of Wymondham became one-way and many people would have to travel down Back Lane, not only my shop but many others were badly affected trade wise, so I decided to lease it to the RSPCA who had been after a shop in Wymondham for many years. They stayed there for 12 years and early in 2012 they agreed to sign up to another 3 year lease, but his did not happen as another shop became vacant and they wanted to move there.

On Saturday April 14th 2012, Colin Hazel drove me and Kenny Cooke to Wroxham Football Club and all the players were so pleased to see us all. Just after half-time Kenny said that we had seen enough and that the club was not the same as it used to be. That was the last time we watched Wroxham play and we have not been there since.

As we drove back to Kenny's house, I told him that my shop had become vacant and as I always took Kenny's sound advice I asked him what I should do with it. He suggested that as I had always done good things the best thing that I should do now, was to let the shop to my chosen charity Star Throwers. He also said it would make him happy and it would also help many people. Three months later Star Throwers opened and one year on it has become Wymondham's most famous charity shop. It has become the first charity shop supporting a local charity for local people.

In this chapter I have written of many things that I have done in Wymondham, but without the support of many kind local people I would have been nowhere.

The reason I have written this book is to give something back. This book will make history. It is the first book written to support this local charity Star Throwers where many good people give their time to help people with cancer. This book is something to give in return to the people of Wymondham who have been good to me.

ID SWEEPERS

Are Proud Sponsors in association with

Star Throwers

Caring for those affected by Cancer

Regal Reunion 2013

CINEMA LEGEND: Les King outside the Regal in the early 1990s

Myself at the Regal with Virginnia McKenna,
star of Born Free

Peter Jackson, a Regal regular

Poorer without him

OUR town certainly found itself on the sporting map last week when the stars came out to salute Wymondham's gentle giant.

It says a lot for Les King that people of the calibre of Dave "Boy" Green and his manager Andy Smith turned up at the launch of his latest book.

People may say it is all a publicity stunt, but let us face it — Mr King does a great deal for the town.

He not only supports local sportsmen and women in their bid for glory but puts himself out considerably to raise money for local charities.

TOWN TOPIC
by Spiggot

He wears many hats and is proud of his sporting roots.

Wymondham should be proud of him.

I would have thought a Wymondham Town Council civic award for his work over and above the call of duty was not out of order.

It is a glowing testimony to the affection in which he is held by so many people, that they supported his book launch travelling

far and wide across the region to pat him on the back.

He is the first to admit he has no room in his life for the prima donna. He calls a spade a spade and you know exactly where you stand with him.

Sport in Norfolk has benefitted greatly from his contributions over the years as a player, manager, sponsor and pure enthusiast.

With the opening of the leisure centre in town this autumn, I would have thought it would be a wonderful gesture to name a hall after him.

Wymondham would be the poorer without him.

CHAPTER 16

My charity events for Star Throwers

In the summer of 2010, the then Mayor of Wymondham invited me to his Dog Show/Funday at Ketts Park. I am pleased I went, because when I entered the hall to visit the stalls, there in the corner was a very special friend, Wendy Winterbottom. I have always called her Wendy Wonder Woman, she is a good swimmer and often frequents Park Farm. She has also worked very hard for Wymondham Tennis Club. She is a good tennis player and has encouraged many youngsters to play. When I saw her that day and visited her stall I bought a 50p dog and a 50p teddy bear, both of which I still have today and carry around in my jeep. Wendy told me that she was a volunteer for a new charity in Wymondham called Star Throwers, that cares for people affected by cancer. I had a walk outside to look at the dogs and I said to the Mayor it was difficult to tell the mongrels from the pedigrees as they all looked the same. Another nice lady who worked for the Wymondham town council gave me a hog roast roll and a cup of coffee. Before I left, I went to see Wendy again, she said that her stall was doing very well and asked if I would arrange a sports event to help her charity. Knowing what a hard working lady that Wendy was and still is, I agreed to support Star Throwers and join her team. It was my first step to becoming the Star Throwers first patron.

I decided to arrange a guest speaker's evening at Wymondham Town Football Club, in early December. Former Norwich City FC Manager Ken Brown, FA Cup winner Greg Downes, boxing champion Jon Thaxton, Danny Nobbs paralympic athlete and myself were the speakers. The club house was packed, thanks to Mick Money's ticket sales. There had been a lot of snow and it was also very icy, but thanks to local builder Andy Mitchell who laid some sand on the path to the club house, people were able to safely get through. Mrs Caroline Hubbard and Mrs Marlene Bransbury along with some other ladies supplied mince pies and sausage rolls for half time refreshments. But sitting near a plate of Mrs Hubbard's mince pies was a 'little monkey' called Thatch, who demolished three dozen mince pies, he did get a bollocking. Wendy and Pat Wooster organised the raffle. It was a very successful evening, enjoyed by many and over £1500 was raised for Star Throwers. The very next morning in Park Farm's swimming pool, Wendy and her friends were discussing the previous night rather than swimming and said 'Les has got off to a good start, we wonder what's next'.

For the start of the local football season, I had my Presidents Trophy game between Wymondham and Wroxham FC. It was agreed afterwards that with the support of Wymondham Town FC, they would play Dereham Town FC for Star Throwers on August 5th 2011 and for my Presidents Trophy. In my younger days I had played football for Dereham and more recently had been a Vice President. I am always treated well when

I visit Aldiss Park, and when I spoke to their Manager, Matty Henman about the game in aid of Star Throwers he was more than happy to bring his team. Matty had played in my team at Wroxham in the past. Over 400 people came to watch the game and Mick Money who had done so much for local football sponsored the game. Former Norwich City FC player, Greg Downes kicked off and the game was refereed by John Seach. John has always been very good to me, refereeing my charity games. John and my friend Richard Gostling are two of the best referees in local football. My friends, Caroline Codd and Mrs Kirby organised the raffle. What a great advert this was for local football and as the game was so well supported, it was good for both teams.

Even though Wymondham had beaten Dereham I did ask Matty if he wanted a re-match the following year on Friday 27th July, to which he said yes. Over 350 people came that day and Wymondham beat Dereham 3-1 to retain the President's Trophy. This game was kindly sponsored by David Smith of Hi Span Ltd. Sharon, kindly as always, made sure that both teams had something to eat after the game. Over £1000 was raised from both games for Star Throwers.

That season Dereham won their league and have now moved up to the Ryman North League. When you visit Dereham FC you are always made welcome and in my opinion the hospitality is the best you can get in local football. They have a hard-working committee, of whom some it seems have been there for years. The Barnes family has supported the club for years. Dereham Town FC has set a fine example in local football.

After the success of the first football game, I was asked if I could do the same with cricket. Hardingham Cricket Club agreed to help. In April 2012 my friend Tony Selby brought a Norfolk Select Team to play at Hardingham. Tony had been a good cricketer and was well respected in Norfolk cricket. I said to Tony that I thought his team should include Daniel Martin, Sam Athurton, Ben Shearing and his lad Matt. Tony replied "who's picking this team?" He did put a good side together with several Norfolk players taking part but the star of the day was William Rogers, son of Norfolk Captain, Carl Rogers. William, at just 12 years of age, hit his first six and scored his first 50 runs at a higher level. The game was well supported and Wendy 'Wonder Woman' was there with her raffle. The game was kindly sponsored by Mark Wilkinson of MW Surfacing Ltd. Tony Selby's team won and a good buffet was enjoyed by all players and spectators.

In early 2013, the new Hardingham Chairman, Dale Watson rang me and it was agreed that on April 21st we would have our charity match for the President's Trophy again, against Tony Selby's Select Team. Dale had helped get the pitch ready at Lords for the England Cricket Team so he was well qualified to get the wicket ready for our match at Hardingham. For weeks before my game the weather was cold and wet and I was rather worried in case the game would not take place, Fortunately the day before the game, the rain stopped and the sun came out. The sun was still out on the Sunday and this was the beginning of our long hot summer. The game was well supported and Wendy 'Wonder Woman' was there yet again with her raffle tickets. Hardingham did beat Tony Selby's Norfolk Select Team to win the President's Trophy. All of the players said that the tea buffet was probably the best in Norfolk Cricket. Over £1000 was raised from the two games. This match was once again kindly sponsored by Mark Wilkinson of MW Surfacing Ltd.

Our guest speakers evening along with the two football matches and two cricket games were well supported. What next? It did not take me long to make up my mind, as in January's Let's Talk magazine my friend Derek James wrote an article about myself and the old Regal Cinema and how on June 29th it would have been closed for 20 years. Several people had read the article and suggested my next event for Star Throwers could be a Regal Re-union. After meeting with my advisors, Colin Hazel of Hazel's Butchers and Ivan (Shorty) Stubbings as well as Myrtle Channon who had been a great help to me during her 25 years at The Regal, it was decided that we would hold a Regal Re-union and it was only fair to hold it at the football club, as they had supported my charity events in the past. Shorty agreed to be in charge of the barbecue and his company ID Sweepers would kindly sponsor the event. Colin said that he would give 100 sausages and beefburgers. Myrtle's son Owen said that he would organise the disco. Even Thatch said he would give £50 towards the cost of the bread rolls but he never did offer to pay for all of Mrs Hubbard's mince pies that he nicked previously! My son, Sean said that he would put together a DVD so that we could have a film show. So on June 29th 2013, as they say in boxing we were ready to rumble. All we needed was good weather and once again someone above was looking down on us as it was a lovely evening. By 9pm there were as many people outside as there were in the club room. There was a long queue at Shorty's barbecue. Owen's disco was a success and Caroline Codd took over £350 on the raffle. Myrtle was kept busy as was Harvey and his staff behind the bar, and I met up with many people I had not seen for quite a few years. I was really pleased that so many people had turned out and given me their support. The event made over £800 for my charity Star Throwers and in hindsight it was the right decision to hold the event at the football club.

Barry Martin, Colin Hazel, myself, Wendy Winterbottom, & Dale Watson at Hardingham

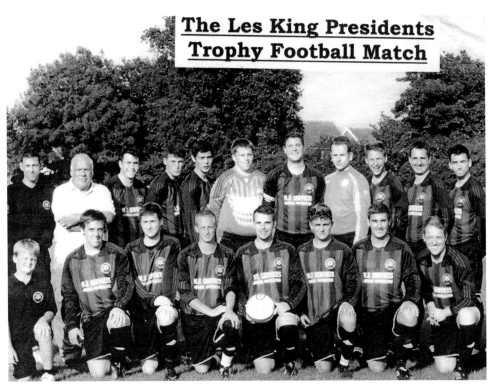

The Les King Presidents Trophy Football Match

Les King's President's Trophy football match

Colin Hazel, Steve Taylor, Dick Bulcock & Kenny Cooke at my Guest Speakers Evening

Les King with the Wymondham team before the President's Trophy victory

Action from the Les King President's Trophy match between Wymondham and Dereham

Lady Wendy 'Wonder Woman' supporting a charity cricket match for Star Throwers and Mark Wilkinson of MW Surfacing presents a cheque for Star Throwers

Both teams line up after the game

Charity cricket match in aid of Star Throwers

LES KING PRESIDENTS TROPHY

Charity Cricket Match

Sunday 21st April at 1pm at Hardingham

V

TONY SELBY'S

NORFOLK SELECT

Match kindly sponsored by  Surfacing Ltd

All proceeds to Star Throwers Cancer Charity

Front cover of programme

The Les King Presidents
Trophy Charity Football Match

WYMONDHAM V DEREHAM

Friday 27th July
K.O at 6.30pm

All proceeds to Star Throwers Cancer Charity

Front cover of programme

CHAPTER 17

Star Throwers
Caring for those affected by cancer

Star Throwers was started in 2009 by GP and Oncologist Dr Henry Mannings. The premises are situated at Melton Road, Wymondham. When you arrive, you are greeted by a volunteer who will make you a cup of tea or coffee and try to help you. Dr Mannings is supported by clinical nurse Tina Martins. I call this lady the special one as she is always so busy. The general manager is Steven Ho, a good snooker player and he is always busy helping people who visit Star Throwers.

The charity is also very fortunate to have a team of wonderful volunteers most of whom have, in some way, been affected by cancer or having lost a loved one. These good people are there because they wish to help. Star Throwers relies completely on the generosity of people and organisations who support and help to improve the well being of those affected by cancer.

Star Throwers motto is a quotation taken from a book: *After a heavy storm a boy walked along the beach throwing the stranded starfish back into the sea. A man watching shouted "There are too many of them, it won't make any difference." As the boy threw another starfish back into the sea, he smiled and replied "it made a difference to that one."*

You will have read of my charity events in the last chapter, and when I became the first patron and became more involved in my shop, which was King of Sport, then I leased the shop to the RSPCA in 2012, they left and I knew that Star Throwers had always wanted their own charity shop. On the Monday morning when I was swimming at Park Farm I told Wendy Winterbottom that Star Throwers could have my shop. She was so pleased that she said we would hold a meeting in one hour with Dr Mannings. I agreed for the first year I would not want any rent and I would get twenty friends of mine to give £10 a month for the first year to help with the shop. It took me just three days to get the support of these people, top sportsmen also gave their support and visited the shop.

The shop has now been open over a year and has become the best charity shop in Wymondham because it supports a local charity for local people. The reason I have written this book is to thank all the kind people and hard working volunteers who support Star Throwers.

The money from every book sold will go to the charity. I have been Chairman, Sponsor, and President of many clubs but in 2011 when I became Star Throwers first Patron it was the best award and honour I have ever had.

Peter and Anne Steward (right) present Dr Henry Mannings, founder of the Star Throwers cancer charity, and supporters Jo Hilton, Les King, Maureen Walters and South Norfolk councillor David Bills with a cheque for £250 at the Wymondham Day Centre

Emily Parr, Danny Nobbs, Steven Ho, Iwan Roberts and myself
at the Charity Shop's Xmas Fayre 2012

Founder of the Star Throwers charity Dr Henry Mannings, Les King, and Tina Martins, Star Throwers Co-ordinator at the opening of the new shop in Wymondham

Official opening of the Star Throwers shop

Community Fund gives £500

Established several years ago, the council's Community Fund invites donations and raises money through fundraising events.

Left to right Dr Henry Mannings, Les King and Town Mayor Robert Savage.

Each year the Mayor nominates one or more organisations which will benefit. At the Annual Mayor's Reception, Town Mayor Councillor Robert Savage presented Mr Les King and Dr Henry Mannings from the Wymondham-based cancer relief charity Star Throwers with a cheque for £500, which he had raised during his year in office. Cllr Savage said he was delighted to be able to give some money to Star Throwers and acknowledged their good work for cancer sufferers and their carers.

Steven Ho, Maureen Walters, Rod Webster, Pat Wooster, Rosa Musgrove and myself working at Star Throwers

My King of Sports books must be the best in Norfolk, there are many whose names are mentioned who are no longer with us, but many who took part in sport will always be remembered. Since I wrote my books I have become a life member of ten sports and other clubs, I am also a member of the cinema veterans association and do have a bus pass so I do not have to spend much money. I did run the Regal cinema for about 30 years, all those who supported me then and my staff over those years did show their loyalty last June 2013, many supported my Regal Reunion Charity event. I did open the Chapel Road fete, it was our best yet, I also opened the Macmillan cancer fete in Attleborough which was well supported. I was invited to Hassingham House in Hingham, this building is built on Haylocks meadow where I played football when I was a boy. I was honoured to cut the tape to open the new M.S care unit relaxation room. Manager Sally Lee and her staff all work hard to make sure all the tenants are well looked after at Hassingham House. There are many kind people who have supported me and worked hard to help support their own charities caring to help others. They deserve credit and thanks.

My long time friend Billy Mann at Wood View Mushrooms, (the best mushrooms in Norfolk) when I opened their new canteen, also their tea lady, Jane (Mrs Ladder)

Myself and manager Sally Lee, cutting the tape at Hassingham House, Hingham

My Wife Anita with Grandchildren William and Amy and their mum Nickie

The Regal Football team's last charity game was against Radio Broadland. I'm number 77, so I didn't get a game. See how many well-known players you can pick out.
The Regal's team was captained by Duncan Forbes.

Left to right: my son Ian, Anita my wife, yours truly and my son Sean in the Regal foyer at the 50th Anniversary Evening on Monday March 5th 1990

Originals

Larger-than-life character Les King has many claims to fame, but he's proudest of his achievements raising thousands of pounds for charity. Reporter **David Bale** met him at his favourite spot, the Park Farm Hotel in Hethersett, where he's treated like royalty.

Former boxer and cinema manager Les King has many claims to fame. He's been known as Norfolk's 'King of Sport' and was once voted the biggest personality in Wymondham since Robert Kett.

But his proudest achievement is his work with charities.

And being patron of the Star Throwers charity, which supports people with cancer in Wymondham, is his biggest honour.

When I met him at his home from home, the Park Farm Hotel in Hethersett, he was wearing his chain as patron.

He said: "I went to the mayor's civic reception in Wymondham once, and I was wearing my chain, and he was wearing his. But the better chain was mine as patron of Star Throwers.

"I have done five events for them including a 10-mile swimming race. I think it's an honour to be patron of the charity."

He's also just been re-elected for the 28th year as chairman of the Friends of Chapel Road handicapped school in Attleborough. He has organised many charity events for the school and walked from London to Norwich and along the Peddars Way both ways to raise money.

Charity work is proudest achievement

Re-run of King's cinema reign

DEREK JAMES looks at a special charity event today to mark 20 years since the silver screen dimmed in a local town.

Twenty years ago "His Majesty: The Picture House Man" switched off the lights at his cinema and walked away... it was the end of King's reign at the Regal. It was the final picture show.

During his time at the Wymondham cinema Les King became the most colourful, larger-than-life characters ever to have run a picture palace in the whole of East Anglia who pulled some extraordinary publicity stunts.

113

It's disco time for those Regal kids

HERE is a message for Shortie, Sparky, Snaggy, Flip, Hot Rod, Cuffy, Dizzy, Killer, Brillo, Ginger, Oz and Butch. Not forgetting Muffley, Puddy, Meaty, Ally and Milky.

They were just a few of the thousands of kids who were members of the smash hit Regal Disco at Wymondham. One of the most amazing clubs of its kind in Norfolk.

And now it's reunion time. Big Les is looking for all those boys and girls for a disco party — 30 years on.

Remember Les King? Who could ever forget him.

REGAL CAFE
DISCOTHEQUE

REGAL CINEMA

WYMONDHAM

Manager : L. G. KING

Phone — Wymondham 2148

Cinema — Open 7 pm Nightly
Matinee Saturday at 2 pm

DECEMBER PROGRAMME

K. WHITEHAND

41 MARKET STREET, WYMONDHAM.

SPECIAL GUEST: Right, disco regular, Bo. Left, one of the flyers advertising the Regal Cafe Discotheque.

Rock on: Les King, who is organising a grand reunion of the smash hit Regal Disco at Wymondham

114

Honouring the picture house king

They called him "His Majesty: The Picture House Man" and they travelled from far and wide to enter his magical kingdom.

Those who stepped into the Regal at Wymondham walked into a world created by ex-boxer Les King, the most colourful cinema boss in the land.

Although the Regal has long gone, the Regal Experience Group now puts on classic Sunday afternoon cinema shows which hundreds of people look forward to,

And they have just made Les an honorary life member. It was down to him that the cinema stayed open for almost 30 years longer than it should have done.

When the place was built and opened in 1937 by Douglas Bostock, the architect was instructed to design a building that would last 25 years.

That is exactly how long it remained open until its closure on June 17, 1962, with the aptly titled movie For The First Time.

But that wasn't the end of the Regal.

It reopened in 1965 and a year later Les was appointed manager after the owner had advertised for somebody

King's reign: Les King dons a USAF officer's hat and sits in a wartime jeep at the showing of Memphis Belle at Wymondham's Regal Cinema.

who could "maintain strict discipline" with any potential troublemakers.

Big and burly Les was the only man for the job. One of the biggest characters who ever walked the streets of Wymondham, they all respected him.

Numbers grow at the Wymondham Golf Society

1984

WYMONDHAM Golf Society held its third ever meeting on Monday, at the Barnham Broom course.

Since the group was formed in March membership has steadily grown, and is fast approaching the 30 mark.

And there were several new faces among the 17 players who teed off for the 18 hole Stableford competition.

The winner was Mr G. Abbas with a score of 46 points, second Mr B. Sanderson, 41 points and third Mr L. Wright, with 39 points.

The society will be holding a meeting at the Cock Public House in Wymondham on July 30 at 8pm, when new members are welcome to attend.

They plan a whole day match as their next event, in September.

● Picture: Chairman Les King tees off on Monday evening at Barnham Broom.

116

BOOK KING: A big name in the world of local sport, Wymondham personality Les King is now aiming to be the top in writing circles.

Launching his third book, King

of Sport 3, at Wymondham Snooker Club this week, it was Les's turn to get a helping hand from the stars he has supported over the years.

Les is chairman of Norwich

Lads Amateur Boxing Club and also holds many honorary positions in local football, cricket and darts.

He is pictured at the launch surrounded by, from left, Bryan

Gunn, Duncan Forbes, John Ottaway, Cassie Jackman and Jon Thaxton from the world of sport.

Picture: DENISE BRADLEY

In the swing with... Les King

SIDE VIEW

Les has transferred his weight correctly towards his back foot, and has performed a nice one-piece take away. Les would improve by adding more knee flex and he has also developed a closed clubhead as the leading edge of the clubface is facing the ground.

This frame shows Les in his full backswing. We can see that Les has a very short backswing.

This is due to the incorrect wrist hinge as Les has worked his left hand too much under his right hand, preventing him from completing the wrist hinge. This is also the reason for the closed clubhead position.

At impact Les has kept very consistent with his spine shape from set-up, which helps to keep his head in a steady position. Les finds it a big challenge to turn his hips towards his target, especially after undergoing a hip replacement within the last 18 months.

Famous faces: Englebert Humperdink, Les King and Tony Weston at the Washington Club

In 2012, Engelbert is preparing for the biggest gig of his life – back in the Swinging Sixties he was sipping champagne with Les "Mr Wymondham" King and singing at an intimate Norwich club.

Here we have Engelbert Humperdinck when he starred at the Still-talked about Washington club with two of the great characters who worked there – Les King and Tony Weston.

"He was a nice chap with a good voice," recalled Les after hearing that Englebert, one of the great survivors on the international music scene, is to represent the UK at the Eurovision Song Contest.

Les is boxing clever to help children with special needs

📷 SNAPSHOT

Our latest nomination for the 2006 Evening News Local Heroes Awards is Les King who has given a lifetime's service to local boxing enthusiasts and raised a lot of money for children with special needs.

He's a familiar face in sporting circles, but what many may not know is that he has also spent many years raising money for children with special needs.

Les King has been nominated in the Community Champion of the Year category of the 2006 Evening News Local Heroes Awards, sponsored by Flybe.

His nominator, Alan Western, of Greenborough Road, Norwich, said Mr King, from Browick Road, Wymondham, had given a lifetime's service to the boxing section of Norwich Lads' Club.

After being eliminated in the preliminaries of Jack Solomon's novice heavyweight competition at the Empire Pool, Wembley, he too retired. But he did knock out Dereham's Ray Bracey, no mean opponent, in the last tournament ever held at the WI Hall.

Since those days, Les has sponsored several well-known local boxers and in the 1970s even staged a tournament at the Regal disco club, where he was manager. Today the "King of Sport" is chairman of the Norwich Lads Club and president of the Eastern Area Ex-Boxers Norwich District Association.

But he will never forget the day he stepped into the ring with Ginger Sadd. About two years after that John Knight began to promote regular dances at the WI Hall, featuring the country's top trad jazz bands. And whom did he employ as a bouncer? The awesome King!

Star Throwers News and Events Blog

After a heavy storm, a boy walked along the beach throwing the stranded starfish back into the sea. A man watching shouted "there are too many of them - it won't make any difference", as the boy threw another starfish back into the sea, he smiled and repled 'it made a difference to that one.!"

Tuesday, 14 May 2013

Star Throwers Patron Les King
A big personality with
an even bigger heart

Since last August we have been lucky and proud to have Les King as a patron of Star Throwers. Known as Norfolk's 'King of Sport', back from his days as a boxing manager and owner of Olympic Removals, Les is a local celebrity in Wymondham with an indomitable enthusiasm for the community.

He is currently the chairman of the Friends of Chapel Road Special Needs School in Attleborough and also the life president of Wymondham Town and Wroxham FC, as well as life patron of Norwich Lads' Club, where he boxed aged 17, and chairman of Norwich and District Ex-boxers' Association.

Knowing all this, it makes it all the more humbling for us to read in his recent interview in the local paper that Les considers being patron of Star Throwers his biggest Honour!

We feel very fortunate to have such a wonderful patron. In the past year Les has helped Star Throwers immensely through his fundraising, particularly through enabling us to have our first ever charity shop last August, and his successful charity cricket match last month. As well as this, though, Les has constantly spread the word about Star Throwers' work and next month on the 29th June he will be hosting a Regal Cinema 20th anniversary reunion to further raise awareness and funds for Star Throwers.

Even before he was a patron, almost from our beginnings as a charity, Les has been a fantastic supporter of our work. We're so proud to have him as our patron and through his continual support we have been able to support more people affected by cancer.

Thank you Les, you're a star.

Star Throwers
Caring for those affected by Cancer

Call 01953 423304 I www.starthrowers.org.uk
Registered Charity No. 1127037

The Grand Opening Of Star Throwers Charity Shop

Star Throwers Cancer Support Charity Shop opened in Wymondham in August 2012

I have received much kind support from:

DUNCAN FORBES, KENNY COOKE, COLIN HAZEL, ARTHUR NUDDS,
IVAN (SHORTY) STUBBINGS, BRYAN GUNN, JON THAXTON, MARK WILKINSON,
MICK MONEY, JOHN SMITH, DANNY NOBBS, DAVE (BOY) GREEN and many others

As this was the Olympic year, Norfolk's top sportsmen
helped to promote the new charity shop, including"

DANNY NOBBS – Paralympic Athlete
JON THAXTON – Former British Boxing Champion
KEN BROWN – Former Norwich City Manager
GREG DOWNS – Former Norwich City & FA Cup Winner
JOHN OTTAWAY – England Record Bowls Player
TONY SELBY – Norfolk's 'Mr Cricket'
BARRY PINCHES – Norfolk's Top Snooker Player

The shop is also being kindly supported by

MONEY PROPERTIES • MONEY LETTINGS • COLINS BUTCHERS • TONY SELBY
MW SURFACING LTD • HAZEL BUTCHERS • BARRY MARTIN • STATION BISTRO
SIMON CASTON • JS ASPHALT • DAVID GREEN • MICHAEL ARMSTRONG
ID SWEEPERS • ARTHUR NUDDS • KENNY BUCKENHAM SCAFFOLDING
LES DAWES • WOODVIEW MUSHROOMS • CAROLINE HUBBARD
CAROLINE CODD & PAULINE KIRBY • POSTMILL GARAGE • PAUL GARDINER
PAUL HAWKINS • CHRIS GREEN • FITNESS EXPRESS, PARK FARM HOTEL

STAR THROWERS ARE HAPPY TO ACCEPT DONATIONS FOR THE SHOP
AT 30 Melton Road, Wymondham NR18 0DB